SUCCESS REDEFINED

HOW TO LEVERAGE YOUR NATURAL TALENTS TO BECOME LIMITLESS!

LEILA SINGH

SUCCESS REDEFINED
FIRST EDITION

© 2015 LEILA SINGH

ISBN 13: 978-1517067779

PUBLISHED BY:
10-10-10 PUBLISHING
MARKHAM, ON
CANADA

Contents

For my Mum & Dad,
who inspired me to be the person that I am…

Testimonials

"Authenticity can be difficult to pick up in an individual, and it takes time to realize how it lives in a person. Having known Leila for over 10 years, I can guarantee it is very much alive and kicking in her. It's alive in everything she does, from her healthy eating to the way she executes her job with tenacity, creativity and fairness. This also drives her passion for life and the way that she spreads that passion to others to excel. Her infectious, even contagious, nature is a tour-de-force, and one that will help you drive towards your end goals, whatever they may be."

Bill Jordan – EMEA Account Director.

"I have known Leila for over 7 years and can clearly see that she excels both personally and professionally. Leila is a very passionate and highly motivated person, radiating a positive 'can do' attitude that is infectious, demonstrating her abilities to empower others to reach their potential.

As a transformational coach, Leila was a source of inspiration that helped me move faster and further towards my goals. The techniques I learnt during our sessions really helped me overcome the self-doubt that was holding me back. I always walk away from a session with Leila feeling, energized, positive and armed with a confidence that I can execute in the areas that make a difference and drive me to realizing my personal and professional goals."

Jason Brown, Alliance Business Manager, EMEA.

"I have worked with Leila in a professional capacity for around four years, and have always found her to be warm and enthusiastic, with an underlying laser-sharp focus to deliver a positive outcome to the client. In parallel we've had an open dialogue, whilst she has been developing her coaching program; during this period I have really seen her enthusiasm for developing people crank up a number of gears!

"I have personally participated in elements of the program and can fully endorse Leila's approach; she has a relaxed style of engagement and a strong level of authenticity, both personally and professionally. I wish her every success with the venture and look forward to seeing her on stage encouraging others to reach their full potential....please don't forget my signed copy of this book Leila!!"

John Phillips, Client Director.

"Having worked with Leila for over 10 years, I can say with confidence that she is a talented and highly driven motivated individual, who consistently invests 100% passion, focus and enthusiasm to whatever she puts her mind to. Leila is an inspiration to others with her track record of both personal and professional success, and applies her optimistic can-do attitude towards any challenge she faces. Leila's warm and friendly style creates a comfortable environment for others to engage, enabling Leila to identify and develop potential."

Mathew Llewellyn, EMEA Sales Director.

"Leila is a wonderful, enthusiastic, hardworking and passionate individual who strives for success.

In the time that I have known her both professionally and personally, I have seen that she is determined, committed and very professional."

Simon Gupta, Senior Finance Manager, Strategic Planning & Control, Information Systems.

"I have known Leila for over 25 years. Leila has always been kind, supportive and honest. She has consistently been very highly driven, and I have seen her tenacity and dedication applied since she was at school and subsequently in her career and personal life.

Leila is the consummate professional and will dedicate her time, energy and discipline in everything she invests in. She is bright, very hardworking and also has a great sense of fun. She has the ability to apply herself to every situation and with the same level of commitment, diligence and motivation.

I have no doubt that Leila will be highly successful in her pursuits to coach anyone - from someone who is very senior in their career to someone who may have just begun their professional career path. Leila will provide honest as well as professional and practical guidance and will be a tremendous source of inspiration. She will inspire, lead and encourage - attributes she has demonstrated and applied in her own successful career and personal life."

Deven Vyas, Solicitor, Head of Client Development at City law firm

"I got to know Leila almost 20 years ago when she joined my team in the early stages of her finance career. Leila has always demonstrated a highly focused, driven and tenacious approach to both her personal and professional life. She exudes enthusiasm and passion in anything she puts her mind to, and is always willing to take herself out of her comfort zone. I have watched Leila progress through her career, taking on many challenges along the way, and overcoming hurdles with determination. Leila always sees the best in any given situation, and her warm and personable style makes her a pleasure to be around."

Chandresh Shah, Head of Finance.

"It has been my pleasure to work with Leila over the past twelve months, and I have found her to be open, honest and engaging. We have worked on a number of complex projects and her professional approach has being invaluable, providing insightful feedback, challenging the status quo and delivering on her commitments in a timely manner. She is motivated to be successful, and that energy certainly rubs off, driving new ideas and discussions that produce new business."

Paul Enright, Sales Director.

"I met Leila earlier this year during the Tony Robbins UPW event in Excel London, where we had a brief conversation. Two months later we met again at the Hilton Metropole London, during a day-seminar with Jack Canfield (known from the movie "The Secret' and originator of the book series 'Chicken Soup for the Soul').

We kept in touch since, and communicated on various subjects. What is especially striking to me is Leila's passion, an incredible urge and will to achieve goals. And you might say, "a Busy Bee" who infects others in a very positive way.

She knows to manage her rational and emotional side like no one else. Leila's passion, enthusiasm and commercial understanding are only a few of her characteristics that made her who she is today, a true leader. In addition, Leila knows how to convey these characteristics perfectly to others. A big thank you for the incredible conversations we already had, and for those yet to come!"

René Deceuninck, DR Communications, www.drcom.be

I have known Leila for over 25 years in the capacity of a close dear friend. Knowing Leila for this length of time, I can truly state that she is one of those people who always generates a positive inspiring energy – "a sense of feeling" good, "can do will do" attitude to life, and consistently in pursuit of betterment. With this comes a diverse range of both life and professional skills, complementing her interpersonal skills of being a strong communicator, and consistently diligent and professional in all that she applies herself to. She inspires and motivates through her ability to connect with people at all levels. Leila's array of knowledge on any subject matter that she immerses herself into is a testament to how she then translates this into everyday wellbeing that can be applied to various aspects of everyday life – health, positivity, understanding potential and finding that medium to achieve both personal and professional happiness.

Mehul Patel, Associate Director

"I have worked with Leila Singh for the past 3 years on a number of complex global projects with Fortune 500 companies and public sector bodies. During that time, Leila's ability to isolate and focus on key issues has helped me to deliver outstanding results to my customers, and consequently has become something I have come to rely on."

Barry Taylor, Solution Manager.

"I have known and worked with Leila for almost 10 years now, in a number of different roles, primarily in and around sales and business development. Throughout this time, what I have always admired and respected about Leila is her continual positive outlook on opportunities that she is working on. A lot of this comes down to how she approaches things:

- Planning – She is focused on the 'End Game in Mind' for each meeting so that she comes in prepared and knowing where is going
- Attention to Detail – Recognising that one size does not fit all in terms of approach, and that she may need to adapt her style to each client or colleague she works with
- Personality – She is always looking on the positive side of life, and looking at how to makes things better

All my interactions with Leila leave me looking forward to the next steps with a positive and upbeat feeling, and continuing this for some time to come."

Campbell Smith, Director, Strategic Sales Centre EMEA.

Acknowledgements

In making the decision to write this book, to share my message, and to make a difference in the lives of others, I want to thank my family, friends, mentors and colleagues, for their inspiration, support, encouragement and belief in me. For this I will always be grateful.

To my mum, for always believing in and encouraging me, no matter what I set out to do, and making me the person that I am today. Your strength, courage and your unconditional love has inspired me to take this leap and see where the journey takes me!

To my dad, whom I respect and admire for your work ethic and dedication to your passion, and for the sacrifices you made, to provide me with amazing opportunities.

To my awe-inspiring cousin, Anup, who taught me that hard work, discipline and preparation really do pay off!

To my incredible, loyal friends, all of whom I am blessed to have in my life - You all know who you are!

A special thank you to those of you who accompanied me on this journey, have supported and encouraged me wholeheartedly, with my mission to fulfill my dream of making a difference in the world, and transforming the lives of others; Barry, Carla, Caron, CV, Donna, Elsie, Fran, Ian, Isabella, Jags, Jess, Linda, Mat, Mehul, Simon …

To my mentors, who have brought me to where I am today; Ray McGann & Mathew Llewellyn, who have always been my loyal advocates over the last several years; David Key, for empowering me with the belief that I really can achieve anything, and teaching me the incredible power of NLP & Hypnotherapy (and for recovering my memory for me – life has never been the same); Andy Harrington, for teaching me how to share my message; Jacob Heiberg, for your patience, guidance and incredible coaching sessions; Andrea Hook, your creativity holds no bounds; and Raymond Aaron, without you, there would be no book!

To my awesome PSA family and inspiring entrepreneurs and business owners I am privileged to meet on my journey.

To my clients who believed in me when I was starting out; I am honoured that you entrusted me to work with you and take me on your journey.

To the many inspirational leaders who have influenced my life, including Jack Canfield, Tony Robbins, Dale Carnegie, Steven Covey, Wayne Dyer, Oprah Winfrey, Steve Jobs, Paulo Coelho, Brendon Burchard, Mahatma Gandhi and Nelson Mandela.

...and to those who have contributed to my book; Andrew Jones, Andy Harrington, David Key, Elsie Igbinadolor, Erdero Holland, Jessen James, Dr. Jessica Morrod, Kathleen Lasco, Neil Martin, Tina Gough, a huge thank you for sharing with the world your personal definition of success.

And finally, a special thank you to René, for always being there for me, believing in me, coaching me, giving me a good kicking when I needed it, and for your endless encouragement to keep going with this book, when I was close to giving up!

Foreword

Leila Singh is a force to be reckoned with. She exudes passion, authenticity and energy in everything she does. She is inspiring, and insightful. Her enthusiasm is infectious. Upon meeting Leila, you will immediately observe a highly motivated, driven, determined professional, contrasted by her engaging, relaxed, fun character, and genuine interest in you. She will put you at ease in seconds, and focus on the task at hand within minutes. Her warmth and easy-going nature create an environment for you to engage, whilst her laser-sharp focus and tenacity will ensure she gets you the results you strive for.

Leila is a talented individual who set out to qualify as an accountant in the UK. Since then, she has achieved great things in her diverse career, exceling in all her pursuits. Whilst developing her career in sales within a global IT company, in parallel Leila is developing a transformational coaching business, where she is empowering highly-motivated individuals like herself to discover their own definition of success, to reach their true potential, and achieve their desired outcomes.

Leila has created her own system to achieve success, based on simple principles she has applied throughout her own life, and also with her coaching clients. In this book, you will learn the ideas and strategies she uses to achieve her own goals. This book will challenge you, let's be clear. You may feel a little exposed as you work through some of the questions. That is what Leila is here to do. To get you out of your comfort zone, to challenge you, to have you really search inside yourself to identify your true purpose, what makes you tick, what is holding you back, from getting to where you want to be. As you work your way through this book, you will build upon the foundations of your journey to success – success on your terms – and create a compelling implementation plan on which to execute.

If you are ready to embrace change, to take action, to leverage your natural talents to become limitless, then keep reading…

Raymond Aaron
New York Times Best-selling Author

Definition of Success

- Establish your own definition of success – one that motivates you on a personal or professional level.

- Trust your own abilities and don't live your life to meet other people's expectations.

- Never underestimate the value of hard work, a sense of humor and the contributions of others to your ability to succeed.

Kathleen Lasco, Director, Global Services.

Introduction

"Take the time to think about your own version of success."
- Robin Sharma

Are you motivated to succeed?

Ask yourself, what does success mean for you? Success means different things to different people. The likelihood is that your personal definition of success is poles apart from those of your family, friends, and colleagues.

Success can be defined in so many ways. Perhaps yours is based on what you earn, your career in terms of status, position, job title, maybe your material possessions, your academic achievements and qualifications, your fitness levels and weight, how you look, or how happy and content you are.

So, how is success measured for you? Is it relative to your peer group, your family, your friends, or simply against your own personal goals and objectives, and your beliefs of what you are capable of?

If you were to reflect today on your life to date, in your rear view mirror, what would you see? All the opportunities that you seized, the accomplishments you are so proud of? Or the times that you procrastinated, missed out, told yourself 'later' or 'next time'? How would you feel? Happy, contented, fulfilled? Or wishing you had achieved more, done more, feeling frustration and regret?

It's important to have something to aim for, to work towards; otherwise, where are you heading in your life? Imagine getting into your car, turning on the engine, and driving off... where are you going? Do you have a destination in mind? Of course you do. Otherwise you would be driving aimlessly with no clear end in sight. Wouldn't you therefore apply the same logic in your life?

Your life is a journey, with a destination in mind, a destination that, of course, can be adjusted as many times as you choose.

If you don't have an outcome, a vision in your mind, of where your life is heading, of what you would like to achieve, of where you see yourself in years to come, you may find yourself simply drifting, with no clear goals in sight. Perhaps you find yourself regularly on the hamster wheel of life, not really sure of where you are heading.

All the hours and the days simply blur into one. Maybe you spend all week planning for the weekend. What about the other 5 days in the week? How do you spend those? Perhaps you're busy planning your next vacation. What about the weeks and months in between? Time is our most precious commodity; never wish it away, for the next weekend, or the next vacation...

"Time is more valuable than money. You can get more money,
but you cannot get more time."
- Jim Rohn

Did you set yourself a goal, or maybe several, many years back, or perhaps you set goals annually, as many do at the start of a new year, and then strive to achieve them? And why is it that the majority of people give up on their new year's resolutions a few weeks into the year?

- How are your goals defined and created?
- What are they based on?
- How often do you achieve them?
- Do you review them and reflect on your progress?
- What is your own personal measure of success?

Perhaps you set goals based upon past experiences of your achievements, or on what you believe to be within your ability, or on the expectations of those around you. Do you prefer to set comfortable goals that you have a reasonable certainty of achieving, so every time you achieve them, you will feel great about yourself…? Or do you set bigger goals and really challenge yourself and push yourself out of your comfort zone? And you smash through those goals and achieve outcomes you had never imagined! How does that feel?

And how does the risk of failure make you feel? In fact, what is failure?

Failure defines feedback; it is a reflection of your learnings. However, when you take the feedback, learn from it, improve, try harder, adopt a new approach, it was never failure, but simply taking the feedback and learnings, guidance and experiences to help you on your way. If you never 'do', you never fail; you never learn, you never grow, and you never succeed. If you decide to give up, then yes, perhaps you have failed.

- And are your goals congruent with you, your purpose; do they fulfill you?
- When you achieve a goal, is the celebration or excitement short-lived, followed by an anti-climax, or does the energy and fulfillment radiate through you for days, weeks, even months to follow?
- Do you feel a sense of excitement when you cast your mind back to that achievement?

- Or do you set goals, achieve them, tick them off, move on to the next…with no real sense of fulfillment or satisfaction, beyond the ability to say, "I achieved my goal"?
- Whose life are you living? Yours, or one that meets the expectations of others?

All these questions and more will be explored in the coming pages. You will see that I am asking you many questions as you read through this book. My purpose isn't for you to simply read through this book, with me feeding you facts, stories and a roadmap of instructions. My purpose is to have you stop and take time to really think, almost as though we were having a conversation, about your life, your true purpose, to challenge yourself and your thought processes, to identify what outcomes you really want in your life, and to empower you with the foundations – the mindset, energy and decision-making capabilities, to get you there, whilst at the same time enabling you to identify and overcome your limitations, and creating the tools and strategies to get you to where you want to be. You may wish to write down your answers to the questions in a notebook, to allow you to review them and create your plan to get you to where you want to be.

My perfect outcome is for you to complete this book, and walk away with a deep understanding of what really matters to you and why, understanding that there are no limitations in achieving your ultimate success – whatever success may mean for you! I believe that everyone has the resources within them to fulfill their true potential; let's leverage your natural talents to become limitless!

So, who am I to talk to you about this subject?

Definition of Success

Whilst everyone's definition of success may alter depending on their lense, my view is that success is the achievement of a goal you set out to do that includes a level of challenge. In corporate life this can be defined as achieving sustainable, profitable, growth – for me, however, that is just one ingredient – to achieve this whilst ensuring the development of my team and finally myself is my goal – when all 3 are achieved, that for me is the sweet spot of success.

Tina Gough, CFO, Global FS Outsourcing Account

My Story

It's May 23rd 2015, and I am standing outside the large conference room at the Hilton Metropole in London....I don't know it yet, but I'm about to have a once in a lifetime meeting.

It's a bright sunny Saturday morning, and I'm very excited about what's about to happen. At 09:30, the doors open. With my VIP ticket, I am one of the first to enter the expanse of this room filled with circular tables covered with crisp white tablecloths. I make my way to the front as fast as I can, heading straight for the table right at the front, centering the stage, and quickly choose my seat for the day.

I'm here to listen to the person who has been an inspiration to me, someone who helped me transform my own life – although he didn't know it. I have this whole speech prepared, though, for when we do meet, to thank him.

"Excuse me miss, is anyone sitting here?" I recognise the voice immediately from his videos on YouTube. And I turn to find best-selling author Jack Canfield, originator of the Chicken Soup For The Soul series, standing right there, asking to sit next to me.

He's tall with white hair, and the thing you notice about him in person is his warm eyes and his genuine smile.

"Hello Jack. I...I...I took a leap of faith..."

'Oh my gosh!!... WHAT did I just say?! What happened to that speech I prepared?!

He just looks at me, maybe a bit puzzled now, but still smiling…

"What I mean is, my name's Leila and I have taken a leap of faith in so many aspects of my life…and I put much of this down to what I learned from your books."

"Thank you Leila. It's good to meet someone else who's prepared to transform their life by leaping. I wish you every success in your future endeavours also." And he smiled that big warm smile before turning to the queue of people who were lining up to talk to him.

You see, I always remember one of his quotes that had a profound effect on me many years ago. He said "By taking a leap of faith in the face of fear, you can transform your life!" So I decided that, even if I was unsure in life, I just had to keep leaping and I'd get to where I was meant to be.

Back in the late '90's, I had realized my dream of qualifying as a chartered accountant with the ACCA, and had the opportunity to build my finance experience in a range of diverse roles with some great companies, including a leading Russian steel trading company, a top 6 multi-national law firm (part of the Silver Circle of British law firms) and a global telco.

Typically, in this type of career, it can be considered distinctly suspect to be taking a leap of faith. Rather, more often than not, you would tend to see the majority of professionals being quite risk-averse, and remaining in their professions for a lifetime. So in theory, I shouldn't be here today writing this; I should be sitting at my desk, number crunching. Just as I was back in 2000, working for one of the country's leading telcos.

One cold afternoon in November 2000, you would have seen me sitting in a quiet meeting room. Across the desk is my boss, a super-intelligent Cambridge graduate; quiet, reserved, and quite simply a great boss to work for!

"Leila, I want to congratulate you on your top rating in this latest appraisal. It's a tremendous achievement."

"Thank you Peter, it really means a lot, and it's been a privilege to learn from you… but (pause) actually I want a different job …"

"Oh, okay, what did you have in mind? Maybe moving to another role in finance? We can take a look at that…"

"Actually, no. I don't want to work in finance. I want to become a recruitment consultant…"

You see, I had seen recruitment consultants in the company all the time and I would love to do what they did! I could do a much better job than many of them! I want to be one of the good ones, one who really delivers value to my clients. I would love to be able to match the perfect candidates in the perfect roles! And I have the perfect background; I understand what clients are looking for, as well as the reality behind the detailed job specs, what they really mean, and the skillsets that would fit .

"You're resigning? Have you something to go to? Is it the money? I can look into that, see what I can do…"

"No Peter, it's not about the money…in fact I am taking a 50% pay-cut to move to recruitment."

"50%??? But you're in the process of closing on your new home. How will you afford the mortgage with such a huge drop in salary? Have you really thought this through Leila?"

You can probably tell Peter is a little risk-averse!

"Peter, it's fine. I have faith that it will all work out. If I don't believe I can do this, then why would anyone else? I know I can make this work. It's a huge change for me, a massive risk I am taking, I agree. But I need to follow my instincts, and just make the leap!"

I received many negative comments from family, friends and colleagues. People thought I was crazy, having studied so hard to qualify and now their view was that I was throwing it all away for what was essentially a sales role!

Have you ever found yourself drawn towards taking action, doing something different, yet you find that a little voice inside your head, or indeed people around you, react negatively, question and challenge you, and maybe tell you you're crazy, that you can never do that? And maybe then you start to doubt yourself…

Having taken that leap of faith… on Wednesday 3rd Jan 2001, suited and booted, I arrive at the offices of my new employer, a small recruitment firm in North London. My director, Steve with super spikey hair and a big smile, greets me at the door, and shakes my hand enthusiastically.

"Welcome to the team, Leila; grab a coffee and I'll introduce you to everyone. Then we'll start you off with a few cold calls to prospective clients – you'll promote the CV of our latest A* candidate. Let's see how you get on…"

It was at this point that I panicked, and the little voice inside my head started…"What the hell! In front of this experienced team, I have to make cold calls?! They will all be listening to me; what if I say something stupid, what if I mess up, what if I embarrass myself, what if someone slams the phone down on me?…what if…??? Oh my gosh, what HAVE I signed up to..???"

Irrational thoughts were flying through my mind, as the reality dawned on me. I had signed up to this. I need this job to pay my bills and my new big fat mortgage!! Were the others right? Had I been crazy to make this giant leap into the unknown? It felt uncomfortable…but you know, 'stepping out of your comfort zone is your biggest opportunity for growth.' I knew deep down I was doing the right thing, and that this was a job I could do, and love. And I remembered Jack Canfield's line "By taking a leap of faith in the face of fear, you can transform your life"… so I sat down and picked up the phone.

Do you sometimes doubt your abilities, question whether you will succeed, or worry what others will think if you were to step out of your comfort zone?

Well, that's what I was thinking as I completed my first year in recruitment, and time for my annual review with spikey haired Steve. He's still smiling: "Leila, I am really pleased with your performance this year. You had no relevant sales experience, yet you have done remarkably well. You have been our highest biller this year."

Wow – I'd never have predicted that on my first day in the job.

"What's more, Leila, I really admire how you get people to open up to you. Your candidates and your clients say that they really connect with you and can talk openly with you. I have seen the way you have influenced others to reframe their perspectives in such a positive way, to encourage others to see their real potential, and push themselves out of their comfort zone, just the way you have done yourself."

As I sat there, smiling at Steve, for me it wasn't just about matching people to roles. It was also about encouraging people's beliefs in themselves. Because many of them had to believe they were good enough before they could be serious about taking a new role.

And I'd discovered a way to help them do that – get over their hurdles, make those leaps, and grab those opportunities that they never thought possible.

For example, a few months before an A* young candidate had come to see me.

"…Yes, Leila, I have been working as a management accountant, but it's no longer challenging enough. I love the company, but I am feeling bored, and would love to do something different!"

"Daniel, have you considered a different role, perhaps something which enables you to influence the direction of the business?"

"That sounds great, but I am not sure I am ready for that. I don't have the experience and I'm not qualified."

"Maybe not on paper, but you certainly have the gravitas, skills and have demonstrated potential. And remember, Daniel, you are more than your current job description. Let me make some calls."

A couple of weeks later, I received an email from Daniel.

"Dear Leila, I started that new job today and I wanted to say thank you for believing in me, and encouraging me to take the leap. I still don't know how you managed to see through my negative view and get me to believe in myself. But whatever you're doing, keep doing it! Thank you so much – I love my job!"

Does what you do today fill you with passion, excitement, have you leaping out of bed in the morning; does it fulfill your aspirations?

Fast forward to today, and for the last 12 years I have the good fortune to work for one of the leading global IT companies, where I've used my sales, finance and people skills in different ways.

During those 12 years, I have had many people approach me for mentoring, coaching and guidance, both on professional and personal matters.

If you'd been with me back in July 2010, we'd have been standing in a sunny back garden at a friend's annual BBQ. I got chatting to Chris, a young guy at the BBQ. He was a financial controller at a leading sports club.

"Oh wow, that must be so cool; I guess you get to go to loads of corporate hospitality events, not to mention mixing with the players and their wives! Tell me, what's it like?"

"To be honest Leila, I don't really get involved in the social side of things. I just focus on doing a good job."

"Oh really? Why's that?"

"Not sure really, everyone is really extroverted and outgoing, and so successful. I kind of feel like I don't fit in, that I'm a nobody, and I guess I don't have the confidence to turn up at the social events."

"Why do you feel the need to fit in, when you were born to stand out?"

He reminded me of myself several years earlier. We continued to chat for a while and I made a few suggestions that might help him. And then I thought no more about it....

The following year, we were at the BBQ again, Chris headed straight over to say hello. I sensed something different about him; his energy had changed. We started chatting, and then he shocked me with his words.

"Leila, you know, I really want to thank you, for that chat we had last year. You made me realize that no one is better than me. It was only me who was missing out because of my lack of confidence. No one else cared. I thought long and hard about our conversation. So much has changed in the last year. Nowadays I am out all the time at social functions and I am meeting a whole new caliber of people in the sports industry. You wouldn't believe whose phone numbers are on my mobile now! Our meeting back then really changed my life!"

I was stunned. I barely recalled the chat, until he began to remind of what we had discussed. I hadn't realized that a short chat could have such a massive impact on someone.

As Maya Angelou once said, "People will forget what you said, people will forget what you did, but people will never forget how you made them feel." In this case, that statement applied to both of us.

For the last year, I have been coaching several managers at my company, who want to get over whatever is holding them back, enabling them to identify what they truly want in life, and creating a program to get them there. To get them from mediocre to limitless!

Reviewing their feedback forms has given me the confidence to take yet another leap of faith, and that is why I am writing this book today to help even more people.

You see, it's about you being able to reflect on the images in that rear view mirror in years to come, and feeling happy, contented and fulfilled, knowing that you achieved all that you set out to and more.

And if I ever meet Jack Canfield again I'm going to tell him this story in full, to show him how not only have I been leaping over my fears to reach my goals, but how I've made it my mission to help other people do the same. I do it every day. And it makes them – and me – feel amazing.

As Steve Jobs said: "Your time is limited, so don't waste it living someone else's life. ... have the courage to follow your heart and intuition. They somehow already know what you truly want to become. Everything else is secondary."

So how can you transform your life? What's a system that helps you do that?

Let me show you what I've learned over the years, the steps I have consistently taken time after time to achieve success, and which I have used with others to enable their success.

I have created a system called the Ultimate Success Blueprint™. This system is broken into seven steps:

1) Master Motivation Matrix™; The first challenges your purpose, the 'why' in everything you do.

2) After which we master your mindset and attitude towards achieving results, your Attitude Alignment Activator™

3) Then we explore your greatest asset, your health, your Body Brilliance Blueprint™ and how we can leverage this to enable you to get to where you want to be.

    These are the building blocks, the foundations towards setting you up for success.

4) The next step is your Dynamic Decision Draft™, this looks at taking control, embracing change and having choices – how much do you want success?

5) We then explore your Critical Confidence Construct™, what may be stopping you from getting to where you want to be, and ways to overcome that.

6) We focus next on your Compelling Commitment Creator™, your robust plan, one that will ensure absolute commitment and momentum to achieving your outcomes, and finally…

7) We move into execution mode, your Supreme Success Strategy™ where you take action, step by step towards achieving your desired outcomes.

Definition of Success

"Success is waking up every day to make a difference by being yourself. Discovering and living with purpose, freedom, and creativity to achieve a deep sense of satisfaction and fulfillment in who you are and what you do. To live your purpose using your unique brand of Genius."

Dr Jessica Morrod, Creator of The Genius Equation

Chapter 1
What is your Purpose?

"The purpose of life is a life of purpose."
- Robert Byrne

What IS purpose, what is YOUR purpose, what is your 'WHY'?

Purpose can be broken down into four key areas that, individually, provide you with your 1) Priorities 2) Values 3) Passion and 4) Vision.

Together, they combine to create your Master Motivation Matrix™, identifying your ultimate purpose, your intent for you during your lifetime.

And what is your WHY? Why do you want to do something? Why are you taking action? Your 'why' creates your emotional excitement, the drive and the momentum towards achieving your results.

This first, and most important, point means that you will have clarity on the journey you are taking through your life. That journey and the destination will be a reflection of your true self, and therefore congruent with your personal drivers, your motivations, your mission. This will provide you the growth that you strive for, whilst enabling you with the certainty and assuredness about aspects of your life that are critical to you, and whilst there may be some predictability with this approach, there is also the uncertainty of change, the excitement of making a difference in your life, and the lives of those around you.

Without this, you drift through life with no clear direction or destination, no end in mind. Perhaps you find yourself living day to day, living for the weekends and those one or two holidays each year... but what about all those days in between? Time is a valuable commodity ... wouldn't you want to be making the most of every minute of every day? Perhaps you look around you and see others achieving the successes you strive for, living a life of fulfillment, contentment and satisfaction, whilst you remain frustrated, resentful, even unfulfilled. You wonder how others can achieve so much, or why they always seem to be so lucky, or perhaps you choose to accept that success is only for other people, whilst you accept mediocre.

What's your why? When you know why you do what you do, even the toughest days become easier.

The first point for you to explore is: What is your PURPOSE?

Would you agree that -

- The daily demands of your life are becoming ever more relentless?
- You occasionally (or perhaps often) find yourself stressed, dissatisfied, exhausted or generally unhappy?
- You punish yourself with self-critical thoughts?
- Perhaps nothing has changed in your life, yet you find yourself in a state of listlessness, apathy, stoicism, detachment, indifference, inertia...

You stop for a moment and ask yourself why. What do you discover?

We all have needs and wants, both at a conscious and an unconscious level. The challenge we have is identifying what these are; often we think we know, and we continue striving towards fulfilling those perceived needs, without any reflection. We then achieve our end goal, our objective, or fulfill that perceived need; however, something doesn't feel right. The elation, satisfaction, excitement, fulfillment we anticipated is either short-lived, or it's non-existent. And perhaps we feel deflated, demoralized, demotivated.

In fact, we may give up, drop our standards, accept less than what we may have done previously, just because. Perhaps because the outcome of all our efforts wasn't all it was cracked up to be. Who told us that the outcome would be so great anyways? Perhaps it was that conversation with your friend or colleague, who has invested in the latest Rolex or designer bag, or is driving around in an exclusive sports car and raved about it so much, that caused you to believe you just had to have it. Or it was the promotion or job you yearned so long for, that would provide you the status, the financial security, the recognition, that you believed you desired. And so you got it. Whatever "it" was. And then...then what? What's next? As you consider the next goal, step, action, material possession...based on....?

We all have a need to experience a life of meaning, a life of fulfillment. One of the original thought leaders in this field is Abraham Maslow, who, in his 1943 paper, 'The Theory of Human Motivation', studied the healthiest 1% of the college student population, and created a hierarchy of needs – Physiological, Safety, Love and Belonging, Esteem, Self-Actualisation, based on his studies of the pattern that human motivations generally move through. There have been many theories since; let's consider Anthony Robbins' ideals on this for a moment. Robbins, a leading motivational speaker, has identified six human needs that everyone has in common, and suggests that all behaviour is simply an attempt to meet those six needs.

1. Certainty: this is where we seek to maintain control, to avoid pain and gain pleasure.
2. Uncertainty: we crave variety and the need to feel alive and engaged, where we seek out the unknown.
3. Significance: our life has meaning; we are unique, special and needed, competitive.
4. Love and Connection: where we have a strong feeling of closeness or union with someone or something.
5. Growth: we seek the expansion of our capacity, capabilities and understanding.
6. Contribution: we focus on helping and supporting others, giving back, a sense of service.

Take some time to consider these 6 needs; think about which needs are more important for you, and list them in your own order of priority. Then consider your common behaviours, and ask yourself which of these needs they align to. This is where you will see and understand the congruency between your behaviours and your needs.

We all have our individual needs, perhaps on a different level to those around us, be that our partner, family, friends, colleagues. For some, Significance is greater than Love and Connection. For others, Certainty is critical, or conversely, Variety, the excitement of not knowing what's around the corner. Everyone's needs are different.

Priorities

Have you ever stopped to ask yourself, what are the real priorities in your life? And, why?

To have priorities in your life means that you have focus; you understand what is important to you, and can distinguish between what is important and merely urgent. This enables you to go through your days, your weeks, focusing on those activities that mean more to you, for which you place greater attention, which feature with greater prominence in your life. Priorities enable you to prioritise your activities, your daily rituals, your day-to-day life. Priorities enable you to take control of your life, and the way in which you assign your time.

Without priorities, how can you prioritise your activities, your day, your life? You are likely to find yourself drifting day to day, reacting to situations (urgency vs importance), demands (most likely of others), thereby enabling others to control your life. You may likely have little or no control over your life, as you simply accept whatever is thrown at you at a point in time and focus your attention there. Later, frustration kicks in when you realize that you have overlooked something of importance, simply because you were reacting, and you haven't addressed YOUR priorities.

A great example is this information age that we live in; how often do you check your phone first thing in the morning, for emails and social media updates, and even begin responding to them immediately? Suddenly you find your time being sapped from you before your day has even begun! This is an example of how others are controlling your time, driving your agenda.

What aspects of your life take priority over others? Maybe your career takes priority over your health, your family takes priority over your intimate relationship. Do you believe that you need to compromise on certain areas of your life to achieve success in others? Perhaps to have that successful career you have always strived towards, or to have that body that you can be proud of, you have to forego success in other areas of your life. What is it for you? What do you compromise on; where do you compromise, in your life?

Have you stopped to consider why or how you prioritise one area over another? Think of it this way; perhaps you have sacrificed time with your partner and family, to work all the hours to get that promotion, that payrise or bonus, and ultimately that revered status and recognition. And later resentment kicks in, when you realize you have missed out on precious moments and memories with your partner and family, or your health has been compromised, has taken a toll, all for that status, recognition, or simply, more money. Was it all worth it? The sacrifice, the compromise, the feelings of resentment and discontent? Of course, sacrifice and compromise are necessary in certain situations as a means to an end. However, to what extent are you sacrificing or compromising? Does the outcome make the sacrifices worthwhile? Ask yourself, once you achieve your goal in that area of your life, how you will feel? How will it look for you? And what about the other areas of your life? How are they impacted?

Consider the Wheel of Life. You can download your own copy when you access your free bonuses. This provides an overview of all the areas of one's life. It enables you to take stock of your life, to identify areas that you may have previously overlooked, to give consideration to where you currently are in each area of your life, and to where you ideally would like to be.

So how do you decide where you will place greater importance? What determines where you will spend more time?

Often we confuse our priorities between what is important and what is urgent. Urgency is typically driven by other people's demands on our time, and when it is driven by ourselves, quite often it is a result of procrastination. Contrast urgency with importance; important activities move us a step closer towards achieving our outcomes, be that in our personal or professional lives. As a consequence, and given our time constraints, we often choose to focus only on specific areas of our lives that we deem of greater importance than others, thereby compromising on other areas.

If something is really important to you, you will find a way. If it is not important, you will find an excuse.

Activity

Reflecting on your life to date is a great way of becoming more aware of what really is important to you; the feelings, the thoughts, the emotions that conjures up. Find some quiet space, sit comfortably, close your eyes, inhale through your nose slowly and deeply from your diaphragm, hold for 5 seconds, and slowly breathe out through your mouth. Repeat 3 times. Now you are in a relaxed state. Begin to reflect on your life, your achievements, and your experiences, personally and professionally. As you do this, you may start to notice an uncomfortable feeling within; perhaps that awareness creates something inside that doesn't sit comfortably with you. Maybe you begin to identify areas of your life that you are compromising on, which make you feel resentful. On the other hand, your reflection on your life brings pride, happiness and contentment to you. There may be areas of your life for which you 'could do better', be that over-performing within your career, accelerating up the corporate ladder, earning more money, having more time to nurture your relationships with family and friends, improving your health and fitness levels, accumulating more possessions…

It is critical to recognize the feelings, thoughts and emotions that such reflection generates. These are your unconscious messages (also known as gut instincts) that are highlighting areas of your life for which you are not deeply satisfied or fulfilled. Until you take the time to reflect in this way, you may never understand what is truly important to you.

"You have to decide what your highest priorities are and have the courage – pleasantly, smilingly, non-apologetically – to say 'no' to other things. And the way to do that is by having a bigger 'yes' burning inside." Stephen Covey

- What dialogue are you running internally to justify these feelings, thoughts, emotions?
- What reasons (excuses) come into your mind as you consider this?
- Would you consider doing anything about that uncomfortable feeling, those gut instincts you are experiencing?
- If so, what would you do?
- Where would you begin?
- How can you be sure to achieve change?

If you choose to do nothing, ask yourself why? Perhaps you tell yourself that "That's just the way it is," you're prepared to accept mediocrity, or "I can't," "It's not for me," or…"I'll do something about it some day"; you defer dealing with the reality until 'someday.'

Does your reflection of your life to date reflect the life you imagined when you stepped out into adulthood and the working world all those years ago?

Some day never comes. Imagine the resentment, anger, frustration of putting off what you can do today. Contrast this with the feelings of making a change and experiencing outcomes that fill you with pride, excitement, happiness, exhilaration! And then ask yourself, "Why not today? What am I waiting for?"

Explore the different areas of your life. How important is each one for you? Why? Where are you making compromises? Why? How does making those compromises make you feel? Are you happy making them?

Do you believe that you cannot excel at everything in your life? Have you ever considered that perhaps a minor adjustment to just one or two of your priorities could have a significant impact on every area of your entire life?

Values

A value can be deemed as a measure of the worth or importance a person attaches to something; our values are often reflected in the way we live our lives.

Values motivate us to act in support of our standards; they are a reflection of what we stand for. They give life meaning and purpose. We may possess conflicting values, or prioritise some over others. Ultimately, our values are innate; typically they are ethical, reflecting our fundamental beliefs of what is right and wrong. It would take an extreme situation for us to compromise on our values. Our values therefore influence our decisions.

Without values, unethical behaviours emerge, morals are compromised, and ultimately this results in disrespect, loneliness, and a significant price on one's personal and professional standing.

*"If we are to go forward, we must go back and rediscover those
precious values – that all reality hinges on moral foundations and
that all reality has spiritual control."*
- Martin Luther King, Jr

Passion

Take the time to tune in to your real passion; what motivates
you to jump out of bed in the morning? What puts a huge smile
on your face, and creates an exciting feeling in your tummy?
What makes your heart sing? What drives you towards taking
action and investing energy towards something that you love,
you believe in, you stand for?

Give consideration to these questions, and to all areas of
your life, both personal and professional. Write down the first
thing that comes into your mind.

Following your passion means doing what you love, and
loving what you do! Passion provides you with the driving
force, the focus and the energy, to get you to where you want to
be.

Vision

Where are you now? What does life look like for you now?
How does that make you feel? Where would you love to be?
What's your vision of your life; how will it look and feel,
achieving everything you could possibly wish for?

*"Make sure you visualize what you want,
not what others want for you."*

Vision, like priorities, gives you focus, direction. Visualising enables you to realize your inner thoughts. It reflects your thoughts about your future, where and how you see yourself, your life, your successes. Having a picture in your mind of where you want to be, be it tomorrow, next week, next month, next year, creates a roadmap in your mind, in your subconscious, to enable you to get there.

By investing time and careful thought into understanding what is important to you (priorities), aligning this with your fundamental beliefs (values), and tuning in to your driving force (passion), you will be empowered with the focus and clarity on your ultimate destination, as well as the energy and direction to get you there. What you focus on can change your feelings and your general state in a split second.

Activity

Take some time now to focus on:

(1) a positive experience, such as a great vacation or a celebration... for about 3 minutes, and then
(2) on a negative experience, such as a time when you had an argument or a time when you didn't experience the outcome you had hoped for... again for about 3 minutes, and in each situation, be aware of your state.

When I say state, I mean, have an awareness of your breathing, your posture, your expressions, the feelings inside you, your thoughts and feelings, both positive and negative. At the end of the exercise compare and contrast your state. Take note of how easily your state changes, just by changing your focus.

There is a Hawaiian proverb; "Energy flows where attention goes." So you have a choice, to expend your energy on positive beliefs and thoughts, on solutions to any challenges you may be facing, which in turn generate positive feelings and therefore channels your energy towards empowering behaviour. Or, focus on the negative beliefs, thoughts and feelings, and you will in turn manifest/experience these in all aspects of your life.

Take some time to think this through. Reflect on where you are today. Gain clarity on what you want to achieve in all areas of your life. Create a vision in your mind of how these achievements will look to you, and be aware of the thoughts and feelings you experience when visualizing your achievements; what you feel, see and hear, and just how much you want those successes! What dialogue are you running internally as you visualise your personally defined successes? Consider how you will feel if you don't achieve them.

"I am the greatest. I said that even before I knew I was."
- Muhammad Ali

Review of Chapter 1

1. What was your biggest insight whilst you were reading this chapter?
2. Explore what is your "why"
3. Prioritise your 6 needs
4. What are your Top 3 priorities in your life?
5. Name one thing that inspires you to jump out of bed in the morning
6. If you were granted the gift of a day, to do whatever made you happy, money no object, how would you spend that day?
7. Visualise your life in 10 years time – what do you see?
8. What action will you take now after reading this chapter?

Definition of Success

For years I thought success was something tangible. Money, Cars, Houses, £1m + business. Now I know it's none of those THINGS! Success comes from a feeling of wellbeing, a feeling of gratitude, it's a great feeling and it's formless. You cannot define it with words but when you feel it, you'll know in that moment... YOU HAVE IT...it's FREEDOM.

David Key, Author, Entrepreneur, Coach, Husband, Dad and above all, Human Being

Chapter 2
"What You Think, You Become"

"You are what you are and where you are because of what has gone into your mind. You can change what you are and where you are by changing what goes into your mind."
- Zig Ziglar

With the right thoughts and attitude; that is, your Attitude Alignment Activator™, your happy, optimal state of mind, a winning mindset, your positivity, energy, confidence, discipline, focus, and positive self-talk, you gain clarity of mind, you know where you are heading – you instill confidence, you can achieve so much! It's up to you! In the same way, if you want to be successful, you think of yourself as a success! Your optimism and positivity will attract like-minded people into your life. The right attitude and thoughts will inherently provide you with the confidence to go after your dreams – and achieve them! Confidence is invaluable in enabling you with the tools to get you to where you want to be, to achieve personal growth in your life, and the success you aspire towards. Your only limitations are the thoughts you tell yourself! As Napoleon Hill once said, "Whatever the mind can conceive and believe, it can achieve."

With the wrong attitude; by this I mean, negative thoughts, language and behaviour, it will be challenging, to say the least, to achieve the future that you have created in your mind, of your life and where you want to be. As Henry Ford said, "Whether you think you can, or you think you can't--you're right." This is so true. When you have a negative outlook on life, and your perception of what is around you is tainted with a pessimistic view of the world, of people, or situations, or even your own abilities and potential, this is what you will manifest. Think of yourself as a human magnet, attracting what you think, speak and feel.

Clarity

Having identified your purpose in life, what is important to you, your vision of your future, what drives your passion, aligns with your values, you have gained clarity about you, and your desired outcomes. So, how do you now get from where you are to where you want to be? Your journey will involve a number of milestones, and each will represent progression towards your ultimate outcome. You will have decisions to make along the way, whilst overcoming challenges and taking risks. Would you agree with me, therefore, that you have to adapt your mindset to effectively handle each situation that you encounter? If you are not prepared to adapt, you will face an uphill struggle, situations will appear almost impossible to deal with, your ability to overcome challenges and mitigate risks will be severely impeded.

Firstly, you need to adopt the right attitude, the right mindset. What exactly is a mindset? It's a way of thinking, a habit that you create by repeating something, in this case your thoughts, over and over, at least 40 days in a row, which then becomes a routine. So how can you create a habit that becomes a routine?

Neuro Associative Conditioning is where neurons make connections every time you think or do something, e.g. "I want chocolate" or "I want to smoke." Your neurons connect based on what you focus on. If you then create a 'pattern interrupt' (a term used in NLP), this causes you to refocus the mind, and break the existing thought patterns. A simple example of this is where you are having a conversation with friend in a bar, and another person approaches, interrupts your conversation and train of thought, to ask you a question; perhaps "Would you like a drink?" Your focus is diverted to the question being asked; you consider the question, and provide an answer, then return to your original conversation with your friend. You have been distracted (pattern interrupt), and are now asking yourself, "What were we talking about?" It will take you a few seconds to refocus, but during that time, you are conscious of the fact that you are trying to refocus back on your earlier conversation. In another situation, this is where you would take the opportunity to grab control of your negative thought processes, and consciously correct them by focusing on positive thoughts.

If you want to install a new mindset, or adjust an existing one, you need to identify the 'pull' towards it. A 'push' towards something, such as a change in mindset, will not be long term, as this demands willpower – which never lasts. If you want to quit smoking for example, you have to identify the rationale, the 'pull' for wanting to do so. Find a reason so compelling that the pain of not changing pulls you towards making that change. For example, the pain could be the adverse impact smoking is having on your health, or the fact that no one will date you because you smoke! These reasons may be so compelling that they create a pain so extreme, pulling you towards changing your smoking habit. The pull creates a new mindset that will last forever.

So how do we apply this to a change in mindset? This is where clarity comes in; in Chapter 1, we gained clarity on your true purpose, what is important to you, your priorities, your passion, both at a personal and a professional level – you created a vision of where you want to be, something so compelling, and so possible, that you are now being pulled towards it. By definition, you will change your mindset to automatically focus on your outcomes, and as you complete each milestone towards the greater goal, your focus and the outcomes will become stronger. If you remain conscious of your thought processes for 40 days , you are training your mind to think positive thoughts; your way of thinking will become a routine and you will accelerate towards your goals!

Listen carefully to your internal dialogue. When you face challenges, focus on the positives and the learnings from them; do not dwell on the negative thoughts, but replace them with positive ones. Become consciously aware of your internal dialogue, and manage it; replace the bad thoughts with good ones. This will create a habit.

Challenge

You may find it a challenge to be always taking responsibility, and making a choice as to how you react at a given point in time. Often, it is far easier to place blame on external factors. But that isn't taking control of your situation, of your life, and your decisions. That is allowing external factors to control you. If you do this, you become disempowered. How will you ever fulfill all your aspirations? Everything will be based on "luck"!

Life is not something that happens to us from the outside in; life is projected from the inside out. For example, how you feel influences your behaviour. Often we blame others for how we feel; "They made me feel…" perhaps due to something they did or said. Think about a time when someone annoyed you, be it in the workplace, or perhaps in a relationship (partner, friend, or family) and how you reacted at the time. Perhaps you became angry and then vocal about how you felt, lashing out, being rude or unpleasant to that person, or resentful, deciding to treat them differently as a consequence of how you felt. Maybe you became argumentative or defensive, depending on the context of the situation. Now, looking back, did any of these reactions help the situation in any way? Possibly not. But at the time, you were simply reacting to how someone made you feel. What if you were to reframe that situation, and consider that maybe, just maybe, that person's intentions were well meaning, that perhaps they simply failed to communicate them in an appropriate way? Perhaps your perception of that person meant that you reacted in a negative way. There are so many what-ifs to consider. Ultimately, whatever the situation, you still have a choice in the way you choose to react. Consider this: who is impacted by your response/reaction? Maybe the other person. What about you? How does your reaction help you? Does it put you in a positive state? Perhaps it made you feel better initially. In the long term, however, how did your reaction benefit you?

We are constantly absorbing vast amounts of information through our five senses. Out nervous system filters this information; as we assimilate this information, both consciously and, moreover, unconsciously, we begin to delete, distort and generalize the information, according to our unique filters, as we create internal representations.

We have a tendency to focus on what is important to us at any given time, and as a consequence, we selectively delete information that is to the contrary.
We can misrepresent our reality and generalize as we process information, based on our experiences, behaviours and beliefs, easily misinterpreting others' intent.

Our internal representations are subjective, driven by our beliefs, values, our perceptions of reality, our view of the world, and creating an image or an idea in the mind. Therefore, everyone experiences any given situation differently. Your perception of a situation may not be the other person's reality.

For example, you could be at a party with your friends. A fight breaks out between a couple of lads; one is badly injured and is rushed to hospital. It is unlikely that your perception of the incident will be the same as that of your friends. Prior to knowing the facts, you may disagree on whose fault it is, whether the badly injured party deserved it, on who started the fight, whether it was in some way justified or whether one party was deliberately antagonizing the other.

What that means is, for example, someone's good intentions may be misinterpreted as bad intent, simply based on your internal representations, and thereby influence the way you respond to a situation. When we gain control of our responses to external situations, through managing our internal representations, taking responsibility for our actions, we become empowered, in charge and in control of our future.

Wouldn't you rather be the master of your own destiny?

In actual fact, we need to learn to take responsibility for ourselves, for our thoughts, feelings and behaviours. It's not about what happens to us or around us; it's about how we choose to react to any given situation. We always have a choice. So rather than blaming external factors, the government, institutions, situations which are out of your control, and other people, ask yourself, "How do I choose to react in this situation?" The approach to consider adopting is one of an optimistic, can-do attitude. Leaders stand up and take responsibility, whereas victims place blame. Which would you rather be?

You are a result of your thoughts. If you don't like your current results, change your thoughts! Your thoughts influence your feelings; your feelings impact your behaviour. No one else is responsible for your feelings but you.

Perception

What is your perception of yourself? How self-aware are you? The way you see yourself may not be the way others perceive you. Your perception is your own reality. However, another person's perception may be poles apart from your reality.

For example, imagine someone who is in their mid-30's and single. What would be your perception of this person? Would you feel sorry for them, thinking that they must be jealous of all the couples around them, lonely without that special someone in their life, that they are missing out on life, and even social events for fear of showing up on their own? Or perhaps you admire them for their independence, their ability to get out there and make the most of life, travelling, doing things at the drop of a hat, not being accountable to anyone, just living their life and having fun? Your perception of their life may be far apart from their own reality.

Or instead, imagine being stuck on the motorway in a 10-mile tailback. You're now ridiculously late for your appointment, getting more and more frustrated and stressed, and then the car in front of you pulls out onto the hard shoulder and accelerates to the next exit at high speed. What is your immediate reaction? What are your thoughts? Do you start to feel even more frustrated, even angry, at the injustice of what just happened, and maybe decide to do the same thing yourself? "Why should they get away with cutting people up and getting further ahead than me?" Or maybe you rationalize that they have a genuine emergency, perhaps a relative has been taken seriously ill and they are desperate to get to the hospital to see them, or they themselves are not feeling well and have driven through to the next exit to get off the motorway and avoid potentially causing an accident. In which case, you remain calm in the traffic, knowing that at some stage you will be safely on your way again.

This is where state of mind is so critical, to all aspects of our life, whether it be towards our self, our day-to-day activities, our health, our career, our relationships, our family and friends, and ultimately, our success. You can adopt a positive stance or a negative one, to any situation you find yourself in; you have a choice, remember? Managing your state means you are in control, you are managing yourself, to the best of your ability.

Imagine going through your day with a positive outlook, feeling happy, calm and in control, optimistic, enthusiastic about what the day will bring. This influences your entire state, your physiology, from the inside out, as well as your perception of the world around you, your experiences, your approach to achieving your goals and outcomes on a particular day. Your state also projects onto those around you; it inspires an energy that will draw like-minded people to you.

We all have the internal resources to achieve the goals we set for ourselves. It is a case of creating the right mindset to get you there. The question then is, how challenging are your goals, your outcomes? How do you choose to set the bar? And to what extent do you need to adapt your current mindset to achieve this?

Contentment

State of mind is your mood, or mental state, at a particular point in time. In other words, your attitude, disposition, outlook, perspective.

A negative state of mind adversely impacts your entire physiology; the cells in your body react to everything that your mind says and brings down your immune system. Often you can identify a person who has a tendency to maintain a negative mindset, simply by the way they carry themselves, the facial expressions and the limited energy they exert simply through movement and voice. If you tend to maintain a positive energy, and you spend time around a negative person, you will most likely feel drained by the end of the day. As you become self-aware, something we will look at later in this book, you will notice the impact of others' energy on you.

A positive state of mind, conversely, impacts your physiology in a positive way. As a consequence you are innately filled with optimism, and happy, positive thoughts; you naturally see the best in people and in situations, you are upbeat and energized, with a can-do attitude, therefore attracting similar like-minded people, situations, and indeed opportunities into your life. Your positive thoughts manifest within, and with your physiology reacting to your state of mind, others' perceptions of you will be enhanced, people will be drawn to you, want to be in your company; in fact, they will want whatever it is you're taking!

It's important to adapt your way of thinking to the risks and the challenges that come your way. Your state is a powerful tool, and with an awareness of this, and an ability to manage it, you will notice how you can take greater control of outcomes in day-to-day situations. And there will be days when it seems almost impossible to generate a positive state of mind. In this situation, focus on your physiology – this is so important; the smallest adjustment to your physiology can have the biggest impact on your overall state. Stand tall, shoulders back, smile, deep breaths, and your body will immediately feel more energized, getting you back into a positive, happy state. It really is amazing how easily you can control your own state! Your physiology can directly influence your levels of health, so it is crucial to form a habit of having a happy, optimistic, upbeat state of mind, and to consciously manage this.

Your state influences your reaction to a situation or an experience. We looked at this earlier when we talked about our internal representations. State of mind is critical to achieving the success you desire. Once you identify the steps required to get you from where you are today to where you want to be, adapting a focused, positive, defined mindset is crucial to getting you there, one step at a time.

Story

The reaction of many people when first diagnosed with a terminal illness, or experiencing massive impact to their ability to live a life of freedom such as reduced mobility, is to give up, both mentally and physically, thereby immediately creating an adverse reaction to their physiology, and general wellbeing. With this, life can go downhill fast. On the other hand, a small proportion of people understand the significance of maintaining a strong positive, mental disposition, and the overall impact this has on their wellbeing, their feelings, thoughts, and subsequent behaviour.

My fiercely independent mother, at the age of 60, who overnight found herself paralysed from the waist down, diagnosed with multiple myeloma (bone marrow cancer), and given up to 3 years to live, adopted a strong attitude to her predicament. She identified reasons in her own mind as to why it wasn't her time to give up. And those reasons gave her the strength and courage to live almost 13 years following her diagnosis. The majority of those years were celebrated with a good quality of life. And what I learnt during those years is that I absolutely, without a doubt, had no excuse to complain or find fault with any predicament in my life. Why? Because I had everything I could wish for, and for anything that was missing, I had the freedom of choice, and the strength of mind, to go figure out a way to get it.

"Your beliefs become your thoughts,
Your thoughts become your words,
Your words become your actions,
Your actions become your habits,
Your habits become your values,
Your values become your destiny."
- Mahatma Gandhi

Review of Chapter 2

1. What was your biggest insight whilst you were reading this chapter?
2. What is your first thought when your alarm goes off in the morning?
3. In 5 words, how do you perceive your life to be today?
4. Having gained clarity on your purpose, identify the 2 or 3 thoughts you have about yourself, which risk sabotaging your success
5. Describe the "ideal" mindset you need to have, to achieve your definition of success
6. What is the biggest 'pull' needed for you to adjust your current mindset?
7. Recall a situation where you reacted to an event, later to learn that your reaction was misguided. (Your perception was not the other person's reality.) Knowing what you know now, how would react in the same situation?
8. What action will you take now after reading this chapter?

Definition of Success

"For me, success is being empowered to live on your own terms and loving the life you lead. It is having the freedom to decide how to spend your time and the resourcefulness to contribute to the world around you, empowering others to also find their own personal version of success."

Neil Martin – Award Winning International Speaker and Empowerment Coach. www.naturaljuicejunkie.com

Chapter 3
Your Greatest Asset

Ignore your health and it will go away...

Your greatest asset, believe it or not, is your health. Often, we don't value it until we, or someone close to us, become sick. All the money in the world cannot buy you good health. Often, however, we find ourselves sacrificing our health to be the best in our career, perhaps working long hours in stressful conditions...and then spending that money to attempt to cure our ailments which were caused by compromising our health in the first place! Does this make sense? Would it not be more sensible to proactively manage our health, to prevent ailments and disease? Without good health, every aspect of your life is compromised. Ignoring signs of ill health, placing less importance on it, becomes detrimental to you, in fulfilling your aspirations and living life to the full!

Optimal health provides you with the energy to go out and chase after your dreams, to live each day to the full as you journey towards your goals and aspirations, to perform to the best of your ability, and consistently give 100% in everything that you do! When your health is compromised, every aspect of your life is too. Simply lacking in energy to perform at your peak, impacting your thoughts and clarity of mind (e.g. brain fog), an inability to be focused in the here and now (due to ill health, pain etc), and ultimately lack of moderation and focus in managing your health (what you consume, regular exercise etc), will all take its toll on your body, have an adverse impact on you and the life you want to lead, whether you notice it now or in the months and years to come.

Whilst we are typically living for longer nowadays, there is little focus on maintaining a good quality of life. Much of this is driven by advertising, commercials etc, promoting endless products which may taste great, be "healthy" and help us lose weight; however, we often forget that these are marketing campaigns. It's not so much about how LONG we live, but HOW we live, that makes the difference. Often, health is not a critical priority for us, instead it's included amongst a list of other goals and objectives that we set ourselves. It tends to become a priority when we receive the warning signs that things aren't quite right, we become ill, or someone close to us is suffering. Why does it take something so extreme for us to appreciate the importance of managing our health?

Sadly, the importance of health, vitality and wellbeing is often overlooked, in favour of career aspirations, the accumulation of material possessions and spending time with friends and family. Why am I saying this? Because without your health and wellbeing, the opportunity to truly appreciate all these aspects of your life is truly compromised.

Many people sacrifice their greatest asset, health, to accumulate wealth, to build a successful career or business, to "enjoy" life – for example drinking and eating whatever they choose and opting for anything else over exercise … and later come to realize that there is a limitation to how much health they can acquire, using whatever wealth they may have by then accumulated. Money can only buy you good health…up to a certain point.

How would your life be different today, if you were operating at optimal health? How would that look for you, what internal dialogue would you be running in your mind? And more importantly, how would you feel?

When asked about your priorities in life, your goals and resolutions, do your responses reference health, wellbeing and, most importantly the natural outcome of this, energy? And if this is mentioned, is it on the list somewhere and maybe not a priority?

So far we have explored your purpose and attitude, what is truly important to you, your thought processes, your mindset, and the impact of your thoughts on your actions and outcomes. As we get closer to understanding where you want to be in your life, and what success really means for you, what is the most important factor to get you there? What will enable you to stay focused, take action and follow through? That one thing is energy!

Would you agree that perhaps you know what you should be doing, eating healthily, sleeping more, exercising and taking time out to relax and breathe? However, what are you actually doing? The biggest reason for procrastination in this area is often time. You don't have time, you will start tomorrow, everything else seems far more important.

Have you considered how disease and ill health will impact your life, your time and your priorities later in life? And the time you may need to invest at a later date to manage this? Would it get in the way of you enjoying life then? Perhaps adversely impact your self-esteem, confidence and belief in your abilities? In fact, would it impact your ability to think clearly, focus, be creative, recall and apply knowledge learnt over the years? How would you feel when you wake in the morning, not operating on all cylinders? Feeling fatigued, groggy, with aches and pains?

Aliken this to your car, perhaps, as you put it through its paces, clocking up more and more miles. If it didn't receive its regular service, get topped up regularly with oil and water, what would happen? Your car would begin to underperform; it would struggle, deteriorate in parts, and then you would find yourself having to invest money in getting it back to its optimal performance. Prevention, as they say, is better than cure.

Wouldn't it be worthwhile to begin investing time now, in proactively managing your health and wellbeing? You only have one body. Shouldn't you place value on it, respect it, and take care of it? If you don't, who else will? And when I say begin, that's because this isn't a trend, a diet, or a 6 month plan; in fact it's a lifestyle change. To maintain optimal health requires an investment, of time, effort, focus, and possible sacrifice, depending on one's perception and your starting point. And most importantly, it requires taking charge of this area of your life – creating habits. No one else, no technology, no science can do this for you. We looked earlier at the way you think; how your thoughts influence your behaviour, in this case, the way you eat, drink, exercise and take care of yourself.

"Take care of your body. It's the only place you have to live."
- Jim Rohn

Would you agree with me that to transform your levels of health, fitness and vitality to its optimum would result in multiple great outcomes for you? Think: feeling better, looking better, clarity of mind, greater focus and concentration, increased energy, and the ability and strength to push yourself to your max to achieve all that you have ever aspired towards!

So, what do you need to consider? Your Body Brilliance Blueprint™. There are four key areas to focus on, which when combined will empower you to move forward! These are: Eat, Sleep, Move and Breathe.

Eat

The food and drink you put in your body can be the most powerful form of medicine, or the slowest form of poison. And that choice is yours and yours alone. You are what you eat!

There appears to be a popular belief that being slim or of average weight means you are healthy, so long as you are not overweight or obese. I would counter this with the argument that being slim or of average weight does not mean you are healthy, and moreover, is actually subject to what you are putting into your body. If you are at your ideal weight and size, for example, yet constantly ill, be that with colds, flu, aches and pains, headaches, fatigue etc, you are not healthy. You may look great, but as the saying goes, it's what's on the inside that counts!

It isn't 'normal' to have a cold or two every winter. I hear this said so often! A cold, e.g. a runny nose, sneezing etc, is a symptom of your body attempting to detox, to rid itself of toxins, and is caused by a weakness in your body, in one of your body's systems (e.g immune, respiratory, digestive etc). So rather than treat the symptom, taking cough medicine or antibiotics which in turn restricts your body's ability to rid itself of these toxins and actually increases the toxicity in your body, perhaps it would make sense to identify the cause, and treat that. If you body is functioning at its peak, and it's receiving all the nutrition, minerals and vitamins needed for optimal health, you shouldn't get sick.

Do you calorie count? Calorie counting is a popular short-term solution to losing a few pounds. Whilst it may enable weight loss, and you look good, calorie counting does not reflect the levels of your health. Health is all about what's going on, on the inside! For example, you can follow a calorie-counting diet, for a woman an intake of say 1200 calories a day; however, what does that consist of? If it consists solely of processed high-sugar high-fat foods, low in nutrition and high in toxicity, you may shed some pounds, but this doesn't preclude you from becoming unwell and in the process slowly poisoning your body.

Feeding your body with good quality, natural, organic, highly nutritious, healthy fresh food, in moderation, and avoiding processed foods, food high in fats, salts and sugars, and excessive alcohol, will enable your body to rebalance itself and settle to your natural weight. This is all about going back to basics. Eat clean!

Exercise:

A simple experiment you could try, to demonstrate this, would be to cut out all wheat (typically found in processed foods) related products for two weeks, such as bread, pastries, cereals, pasta, and processed foods containing wheat (breadcrumbs, sauces etc), and make notes daily of what you experience during that time – how you feel, what you notice, any changes in your body. More often than not, you will experience increased energy, greater clarity of mind, maybe lose a few pounds and reduce any bloating you may typically experience.

Many of the world's diseases can be found in the developed and developing countries, and can be attributed to lifestyle, and are therefore preventable. This demonstrates that wealth has no control over disease prevention. An unhealthy diet, lack of exercise, along with drug abuse, smoking and excessive alcohol intake, are all considered to be major factors influencing disease.

Story

I apply the 80/20 rule to my lifestyle with respect to what I put into my body. In other words, at least 80% of the time, I will eat only good quality, fresh, nutritious, healthy, natural foods and avoid all processed foods, sugar, wheat, gluten, dairy, etc., and am generally in good health. I don't suffer with colds, flus, and day-to-day ailments of any kind. I recently spent a couple of weeks visiting family in Guyana, South America; here, I ate more in quantity than I typically would at home (3 full meals a day, visiting families who wanted to cook big lunches and dinners). I was slightly concerned that I would be returning to London the size of a house. As it turns out, I dropped several pounds without even trying, which for me is no mean feat! After some reflection, I realized it was down to the simple fact that I had put no 'poisonous' substances into my body for about 10 days. Although I had eaten more than usual, everything I had eaten comprised of fresh, organic, healthy, natural foods, and that included plenty of meat and fish too. There had been nothing processed, no sugars; everything I had eaten was 'real' food!

And what about drinking? We all know we should drink plenty of fresh water, but how much should we be drinking? Studies suggest we should drink as a minimum 30ml of water per kg of body weight. For example, if you weigh 60kg, you need to be drinking as a minimum [60kg x 30ml] 1.8 litres of water daily. This does not mean juices, teas and coffees and squash; simply fresh water. As you begin to adjust your eating habits, you may find yourself craving less caffeine, in which case this would be an opportunity to reduce or cut out your intake of caffeine altogether. Be aware of the sugar content in many drinks, be they fruit juice, carbonated drinks, flavoured waters, etc., often promoted as "healthy" and loaded with several spoons of sugar or even worse, sweeteners! Remember: back to basics. Familiarise yourself with the ingredients on various drinks.

A recommended ritual, to get you into the habit of drinking water, is to have as your first drink of the day a large mug of cold or warm water with a slice of lemon. There are many benefits; it flushes out toxins, contains natural vitamin C, potassium, cleanses the liver and aids digestion, acts as an appetite suppressant, keeps your skin clearer, and is a great way to rehydrate your body first thing in the morning! Give it a go for a week and see how you feel!

It's important to remember that everyone's body is unique, and therefore what works for one person may not work for the other. If one approach to eating works for one person (e.g. juicing, raw foods, fasting 2/7 days, high protein, high carbs, etc.) this does not mean it will work for another. For example, whilst fruits, vegetables and juices are generally marketed as being healthy, for others, some or all of them can be a slow poison and something to be avoided. The same can be said for meat and fish. Some people opt to become vegetarian, as this is deemed to be healthy, and whilst it is for some, depending on your constitution, it may be detrimental to others. So there is an element of trial and error to see what works for you as an individual. However, the basics remain the basics. Think about when you enter a supermarket. Ideally you should be shopping in the first few aisles only – fresh fruit and vegetables, meat and fish. Beyond that, virtually everything else is processed and unnatural. Eggs, oils, and rice may be exceptions, but again, opt for the healthy options; brown whole grain rice over the white processed version. If your budget allows for it, consider organic foods - think about all those pesticides and toxins that are impeding on your health. Many small changes over time will result in huge gains over the long term.

I referred earlier to this being a lifestyle choice, rather than a fad that you follow for a couple months. As you repeat something, be it a thought or an action, it becomes a habit. A habit then forms part of your unconscious and you are drawn to think or do so naturally; it is no longer an effort. So whilst changing your habits in the way I have outlined above may seem like a huge challenge, if you start by breaking it down into little actions, and adopting one or two at a time, they will become habit-forming, and as you experience the outcomes, in the way you feel, how you look, etc., it will become less of an effort and more of a habit. Now wouldn't that be simply great!!??

Move

What I often hear people say is that one of the biggest challenges of exercising is time. Imagine if you could find just 30 minutes a day to be active, to move, to exercise, whatever that may entail; that constitutes 2% of your day!!! Generally you spend approximately 30% of your day asleep. What percentage of your day do you 'waste', doing something that adds no value to your purpose in life, be that watching a soap on TV, surfing the net, checking out what everyone else is doing on Facebook, gossiping about others…and then contrast this with the extensive benefits of being active for 30 minutes every day!

So what should you do during those 30 minutes? Active can be anything you like; cardiovascular exercise, pounding the pavements or training at the gym on the rower, x-trainer, treadmill or bike, strength and resistance exercise including weights and body weight exercise, swimming, walking, be it fast or slow, boxing, sports such as badminton, squash, football, rugby and cricket, or stretching, pilates and yoga... there are so many choices for us all. Perhaps you are competitive and enjoy team sports, or you like to take time out and clear your head by going for a run. Maybe you're motivated by training at the gym with like-minded people who have similar goals, or you like to take in the fresh air with a long walk, or you enjoy the holistic benefits of yoga and pilates. Walking and running outside is free. And if it's cold and raining, buy a DVD and work out in the comfort of your home! There are no excuses. There is something for everyone, however little time you may have.

The benefits of being active are endless; besides looking good, being active improves your cardiovascular health, burns fat, increases oxygen into the blood stream, improves your strength of both body and mind, boosting brain function for example. The benefits to the brain are often overlooked; exercise increases production of neurochemicals that promote brain cell repair, reducing the risk of degenerative diseases such as Alzheimers, it improves memory and brain power, lengthens attention span, boosts decision-making skills and prompts the growth of new nerve cells and blood vessels. Exercise alleviates stress and anxiety, creates 'happy hormones', releasing endorphins! It improves self-confidence and self-esteem, enhances productivity (compared with being sedentary – so get up from your desk and go for a 5 minute walk every so often), and creativity, increases the ability to relax as well as get a good night's sleep. So, exercise is not just all about looking good in that suit or dress!

Take every opportunity to be active. Park your car further away so you have longer to walk, take the stairs instead of the lift, walk instead of drive where you can; these may appear to be small things but it all adds up. Grab yourself a pedometer or something similar (most smartphones have a free Pedometer App nowadays that you can use), and you will see the steps adding up! You may be pleasantly surprised!

"I have always believed that exercise is the key
not only to physical health, but to peace of mind."
- Nelson Mandela

Breathe

Breathing, just like moving, generates increased oxygen into the body, which delivers a wealth of benefits to us; besides feeling energized, increased oxygen eliminates toxins, improves digestion, metabolizes fat and carbohydrates, and increases clarity, as well as strengthening our immune system. Breathing, in the form of meditation or yoga for example, will find you feeling calm and centred, something that is critical with today's busy, stressful lifestyle. Your emotions will be more balanced and you may experience a more reflective, conscious behaviour, as well as improved mental agility and creativity, and an enhanced sleep.

Exercise:

A simple exercise can quickly demonstrate the immediate benefits of breathing.

- Sit comfortably with your eyes closed, maintain a good posture (sitting up straight), take a long slow deep breath in through the nose, and then out through the mouth.
- Repeat this slowly three times
- Then return to breathing normally

- Direct your attention to your breathing
- Be aware of thoughts and feelings, sounds and emotions that deflect your attention
- Acknowledge this and direct your attention back to your breathing
- Maintain this for a few minutes
- Then slowly open your eyes and be aware of your immediate feelings and emotions. You will likely experience calmness and a feeling of relaxation. Contrast this with your original state before you began the exercise.

Breathing enables you to manage your state; for example, next time you find yourself in a stressful situation, perhaps stuck in traffic, take some slow deep breaths, and notice how your state changes, and how you begin to experience a state of calm. As we discussed in the previous chapter, maintaining a positive state is the best outcome for you, and enables you to stay in control of your emotions and actions.

Mindfulness is becoming more common nowadays. This is a state of being in the now. Often when undertaking a task, our mind wanders, perhaps to the party last weekend, that run-in with a colleague last week, the events of the day, that long task list yet to complete, an upcoming event, what we're having for dinner; it could be anything, whether it creates stressful anxious feelings or those of excitement and happiness! The result is we are focusing on the past or on the future. Mindfulness enables us to focus on the now, increasing awareness and clarity, using our five senses to notice what we don't usually notice, in fact placing more control over what we choose to focus on. Energy flows where attention goes. So take the time to decide where to focus. You will attract what you focus on.

Exercise:

This simple exercise will demonstrate your levels of focus. How many times throughout the day do you glance at your watch? And yet, what if I were to ask you, what is the design of your watch-face, how are the numbers represented on your watch? Can you tell me immediately? Are they standard digits, roman numbers, dots, stones, are all 12 represented, or only 4, or just one? This highlights your focus; you glance at your watch to see the time, and miss the other details...

Sleep

Your body needs regular sleep, so that it can rest, repair itself, rejuvenate, and replenish energy levels. Studies suggest adults should get a minimum of 7 hours sleep to ensure our cognitive and physical abilities are not impaired. Of course, some people function at 100% on 6 hours sleep a night, and others need more than 7.

Sleep plays a major role in both emotional and physical health, as well as reducing your risk of chronic disease and supporting your immune system. Studies suggest a link between sleep deprivation and obesity, with tiredness increasing appetite. In addition, sleep deprivation can cause irritability, memory lapses, impaired judgment, risk of diabetes type 2, aches, tremors, and adverse effects on the heart.

Catching up on sleep, say at the weekend, after sleep deprivation during the week, can work on the odd occasion; however, if this becomes a regular habit, you may wish to consider adjusting your sleep patterns in the week. The scary thing is, when sleep deprivation becomes a habit, you can quickly lose track of what functioning at 100% really felt like...

Sleep deprivation has been one of my biggest challenges to overcome. I am a night owl by design, always have been and as such will find myself wide awake and alert into the wee hours of the morning. However, when the alarm goes off at 5:45am... well...no comment. That's when I kick myself and remind myself never to do that again....and so the cycle continues. I certainly notice the difference when I have had a good night's sleep, which usually constitutes 7-8 hours of sound sleep. My mental ability is by far more alert, focused, and active, whereas I often find with sleep deprivation that my brain is foggy, I am slower in processing information and my memory does not serve me as well. Physically, I simply feel in a better state of wellbeing and have bags more energy after a good night's sleep, which enables me to put myself through a rigorous workout. What I have noticed, also, is that the short-term impact of sleep deprivation, particularly mental alertness and energy levels, can be overcome by the benefits of regular yoga and breathing. Whilst I would not advocate regular sleep deprivation on a long-term basis, it is worth keeping this in mind to get you through on occasion.

Summary

I know I have given you a lot here to take on board, and whilst you may already be implementing some of this, it may also seem like a huge mountain to climb; so much to change, so much to think about. You may read this, and dismiss it, because you have tried similar things before and they didn't work. But is that a reason to give up? Think about all the benefits you can experience, even just by starting small? How long does a baby take to learn to walk? 10, 12, 14 months sometimes? And do you write them off, give up on them, saying that it will never happen? Of course not! So why do that to yourself? It is never too late to change. Every second is a chance to turn your life around!

Aliken this to hitting a golf ball; when you hit a golf ball at a specific angle, it will head in a certain direction and travel over a certain distance. If you were to adjust your swing, or the club head just slightly, as it makes contact with the ball, the ball will land in a different location. If you choose not to adjust the club, you achieve the same outcome. In the same way that Einstein says, if you keep doing what you are doing and expect different results – this is the definition of insanity! Therefore, if you want a different result, make a decision to change something. If you want more energy, good health, increased strength, clarity, and ultimately optimal health, begin by making slight adjustments in the direction towards improved health. As you experience the benefits, you will naturally want to do more, and those adjustments will become habits.

Exercise:

And if you're reading this and telling yourself it's too late to change, picture this; You are holding a strip of paper 100 centimetres long.

This paper represents 100 years.

You were born at zero.

Assume the average lifespan in Europe is approximately 82 years.

So you tear off the paper at 82cm and you are left holding a strip from 0-82.

Then tear off the paper at the point that represents your current age.

You are left holding a short strip of paper representing your average remaining years of life.

Assuming one third of that is spent sleeping; how do you plan to spend the remaining years – that remaining strip of paper? Are you accepting of mediocre health, ailments and potential disease, or are you ready to take charge of your health?

It is never too late to make a decision, to change, to improve. It takes one second to change a habit...so what are you waiting for?

Review of Chapter 3

1. What was your biggest insight whilst you were reading this chapter?
2. How do you currently rate your health and fitness levels on a scale of 1-10?
3. Where does health feature in your current list of priorities? (before reading this book)
4. What should you be doing with respect to your health, that you are not currently doing?
5. How do you see you life being different, if you were at optimal health today? What would it feel like?
6. What changes do you need to make in your life today in order to do what you should be doing?
7. What is stopping you from making those changes?
8. What action will you take now after reading this chapter?

Definition of Success

Success means different things to different people; however, I think it also depends on where you are in your life. When I was working my way up the corporate ladder in the banking world, working at many prestigious banks in the city and Canary Wharf, success to me was about goals and attaining them. Having something to measure against! So getting a 1 on my performance appraisal from the General Counsel (top lawyer) was a mark of success. Getting a big bonus, another. Getting a promotion, another mark of success. Being considered for MD; so earning a huge salary, travelling 1st and business class etc., was how I measured success. And this is how I was measured against my peers and in society. However, I always asked myself whether I was happy!! And I could not say hand on my heart that I was.

You see, in achieving success I had to give up so much...in particular my time!!

So I made a decision that to be truly successful I had to give myself time! Time to think, time to ponder. Time to heal. ...Time to enjoy, time to do nothing if that is what I wanted to do, and not feel guilty, time to be happy doing what I want, with the people I want when I want...to do the thing ...that I was born to do. ...BUT also to find out the thing that I was born to do and be the best I can be...so am I successful? I believe I am getting there but I am not there yet. ...I am still finding out the thing that I was born to do - but what I do know is that each day, since leaving the world of banking...each day I am one step closer.

**Elsie Igbinadolor, ACA, Property Investor,
Award Winning Speaker, Mentor & Coach**

49

Chapter 4
To Be or Not To Be...

"It is in your moments of decision that your destiny is shaped."
- Anthony Robbins

Decisions drive outcomes. I used to believe that decision-making came naturally to everyone. In recent years I have realized that this is not the case, and it can be incredibly challenging for many. So I created the Dynamic Decision Draft™

Procrastination

Definition: Procrastination is the practice of carrying out less urgent tasks in preference to more urgent ones, or doing more pleasurable things in place of less pleasurable ones, and thus putting off impending tasks to a later time, sometimes to the "last minute" before a deadline.

"Procrastination is one of the most common and deadliest of diseases and its toll on success and happiness is heavy."
- Wayne Gretzky, Canadian Athlete

If you want change in your life, procrastinating will not help you. You need to make decisions. Making decisions is fundamental to making progress towards achieving your goals, outcomes and aspirations. If you find yourself procrastinating, perhaps you need to ask yourself why.

- What are the reasons you believe you have a decision to make?

- Why are you putting things off?
- Why are you delaying taking action?
- Why, if something is important and urgent, are you not prioritizing taking action?

Contrast these with the reasons why you are not making a decision, not taking action. And then ask yourself, which reasons are more compelling to get you to your outcome?

If you don't achieve your outcome, how will you feel? What will that look and sound like for you? What will you hear? How does this contrast with how you will feel, what it will look and sound like, when you achieve your outcome? Take some time to really consider this, write down your answers and reflect on them.

The reason 'WHY'

There could be several reasons for procrastination, and it is important to get to the bottom of it, and understand the reason 'why'. Because the 'why' is what this is all about. The 'why' is what gets you out of bed in the morning, influences your thoughts and behaviours, pulls you toward something, inspires you, creates the passion within, drives you forward to take those first steps, however small, to get you to where you want to be!

Perhaps what is stopping you relates to some form of fear, be it fear of failure, of success, of taking risks, of the unknown, or of what others may think or say. If so, go back to the 'why'. If your why is compelling enough, this may get you past your fears. Alternatively, once you have your why, you need to explore what is holding you back. We will examine this in the next chapter.

Do you consider yourself a thinker, dreamer, or an action taker? If you are a thinker or a dreamer, that's okay. So long as you remain cognizant of the fact that until you begin...to do, to make a decision, to take action, nothing will change. If you are an action taker, that's okay too. It's likely that you will have begun.

"Begin while others are procrastinating.
Work while others are wishing."
- William Arthur Ward

If you have goals and outcomes, to achieve these, you need to begin. You may believe that you are not yet ready. Perfectionism is often an excuse to procrastinate. Perhaps the time isn't right. Then ask yourself, how will you know when you will be ready? How will you know that it's the right time? If you are not careful, you could find yourself waiting for the rest of your life, to begin.

Without decisions, you have uncertainty of where the future lies. Things may remain the same, and nothing moves forward. Conversely, they may change, without you taking control, without you making decisions. So you find yourself in reactionary mode. And then, you have someone or something to blame, if things don't go your way. In fact, you may be lucky - they may go your way, but that is left to fate.

By taking responsibility for your current situation, and deciding where you want to be, you can influence the end result, through making decisions every step of the way, by taking control of everything that will have an impact on your outcome! Be mindful of the fact that you may not be able to control everything, so to ensure momentum and effectiveness, focus your energies on your sphere of influence, some of which we have already explored; for example, your purpose, and in particular your priorities, your attitude and mindset, maintaining your energy levels, as well as continually expending time on your own personal and professional development, and managing your time effectively.

You made a decision to read this book – because you want to learn how to leverage your natural talents to become limitless! That's a great start; however, we want to ensure you maintain the momentum! So far, we have explored your purpose, what is important to you, how that aligns with your values and vision, and what you are truly passionate about. We then worked towards mastering your mindset, to empower you to move forward, through getting clear on your beliefs, considering the challenges you need to overcome, and understanding the importance of your state of mind. The next area to master was your greatest asset, your health and wellbeing. Here we have talked about four key areas, Eat, Sleep, Move and Breathe, and the importance of striving towards optimal health. Mastering this will give you the energy you need to maintain the momentum, to stay focused, passionate and driven towards getting from where you are to where you want to be.

Taking Control

"You have control over 3 things: what you think, what you say, and how you behave. To make a change in life, you must recognize these gifts are the most powerful tools you possess in shaping the form of your life."
- Sonya Friedman

This is all about assuming full responsibility for steering yourself towards success, as defined by you. With a clearly defined purpose, adopting a strong mindset and generating the energy to maintain momentum, now is the time to take control, take the initiative to drive towards your desired outcomes. This is where you will need to draw on your internal resources, your determination, tenacity and discipline, to get you to where you want to be.

I am a strong believer that everyone has the resources within them to achieve the success they truly desire. Where people don't succeed, there may be multiple reasons, and before blaming circumstances or others, this is where one has to look within themselves, to determine whether the success they were striving towards was really congruent with their true purpose. Lack of congruency is where things begin to fall down. And that is why I stressed the importance earlier of identifying your true purpose – your ''why'.

When you set your mind on achieving something, that which may be somewhat of a challenge, however big or small, be it a new job, a new home, more money, a slimmer or more toned figure, and you focus on it with such passion, determination, taking control and executing on your entire plan to get you there...and it doesn't happen...what do you do? Do you keep trying, or do you give up? The minute you give up is the minute of realization that your outcome was never entirely congruent with your true purpose. For if it was, you would never give up.

Playing the victim, and blaming circumstances and those around you, will get you nowhere. Before you begin to do this, reflect on the reasons for things not working out. What went wrong? What could you have done differently? Where could you have improved? This is where failure becomes your feedback. Take on the feedback and then set about finding a solution. This is your learning opportunity and enables you to develop both personally and professionally. And don't allow others to control the direction of your life.

*"I can not always control what goes on outside,
But I can always control what goes on inside."*
- Wayne Dyer

So taking control becomes a creative process from the inside out, it is about drawing upon every core of your internal resources, to empower you to get to where you want to be.

Story:

Did you know that Colonel Sanders did not begin to fulfill his dream until he was 65 years old? He received his first social security cheque for $105, got angry and, rather than playing victim and blaming society and the state, he began to consider what he had that would be of value to others. He had a chicken recipe that everyone seemed to love. He spent 2 years driving across America, knocking on doors, telling each restaurant owner about his chicken recipe, showing them how to cook it properly. Each time he was rejected, he focused on how to tell his story more effectively the next time to get better results. He experienced 1,009 "no's" before he heard his first "yes"! Would you be willing to accept even 10 no's, let alone 1,009, and keep on going? Determination, hard work, tenacity, and not allowing anything to stop you making your vision a reality, is what it takes to achieve true success!

Change

Become the master of change. Embrace change. You will experience change, however big or small, in many aspects of your life, once you take control and make a decision to move forward. And if you want change, you have to be willing to be uncomfortable, to step out of your comfort zone. To do whatever it takes to get you to where you want to be.

What needs to change?

"Intelligence is the ability to adapt to change."
- Stephen Hawking

You may need to change the way you think. Refer back to the earlier chapter on mindset. Perhaps in the past you have accepted the way things have been, and now you realize you want more. So you may need to think bigger, more creatively, more optimistically, adopting a different mindset.

Perhaps you have realized that you need to change the way you feel, about what others think, about not getting it right first time, about your current situation – instead of feeling satisfied and accepting of your current situation, feeling driven towards change and achieving more.

Maybe you have to change your decision-making methodology. What have your decisions been based on in the past? And why should that change? Was it based on beliefs or fears that held you back? Or on other people's points of view over-riding your own? Or simply on the basis that you had accepted mediocre and not considered that you could aspire towards so much more?

What about your habits? Do they need to change? For example, to achieve optimal health and wellbeing, which in turn will enable you with the energy to focus on transforming your life to where you want to be, you may need to consider changing your current eating or sleeping habits, or your training routine.

Changing perspective will be inevitable. Maybe you have held yourself back from moving forward, whether that be due to accepting the status quo, not knowing what you really wanted, where to start, lacking the self-belief that you can achieve more, perhaps believing your situation was down to circumstance. Whatever it is, you have options; you can adopt the victim perspective, and simply be reactive to situations in your life, blame others for your outcomes and give up all responsibility. However, if you are still reading thus far, I would sincerely hope that is not an option you are considering. Adopt the student perspective; you shift your perspective, but do not necessarily take action. Your mind opens up to what could be, you embrace new learnings, but perhaps you are not yet ready for change. Finally, you can adopt the master perspective, whereby you embrace the change, take control, make decisions, become proactive towards making things happen, and influence others, becoming a thought leader. Which would you rather be?

So, why master change? Because change is the essence of life. Be willing to surrender what you are, for what you could become.

Choices

"Life is about choices; it's not about excuses. Excuses only trap us into believing that we cannot take control of our own lives." - Michael Gerber

Every situation, every opportunity, has a choice. It is up to you how you choose to react. Every decision has an outcome.

Does it therefore make sense to exercise due diligence, weigh up the pros and cons, and give consideration to the potential outcomes, of any given situation, before making a decision? Yes and no; in reality it depends on the nature of the decision, and the potential outcome. If it's a choice between wearing a blue shirt or a pink shirt to work on Monday, well, the outcome of that decision is unlikely to be controversial, or to add risk and stress to your day (unless of course you have a very specific dress code at work on Mondays). On the other hand, if a decision to accept a promotion may result in you needing to relocate to another country, there is much more to consider.

Having identified your purpose, and those things that are truly important to you, you are faced with choices. A common one may be, are you open to change in your life? Are you prepared to change? What needs to change? To what extent are you prepared to change in those areas? How much you really want that change will determine how much you are prepared to put in.

For example, you may believe that you absolutely 100% want a specific outcome, and are prepared to do whatever it takes to get there; however, you make a decision to change your training programme, and not your eating habits. That is your choice; you have the power and the right to make that decision. And of course, you accept the consequences of your decision.

Another example may be that you have decided to apply for a new job, but your mindset with respect to your ability to do that job hasn't changed. You still believe that the other applicants are far more experienced and better suited to the job than you, and that they will never take your application seriously. You have made a choice not to change your attitude; your state of mind, your lack of confidence, will come across in your interview.

We have examined the importance, in fact the criticality, of taking control if you want to achieve success, as well as your need to master change. Many people find change a challenge to accept, to embrace, especially when the change impacts their life in a big way. However, if you want to move from where you are today to that vision of what success look, feels and sounds like for you, change will be inevitable. So accepting change will come down to how much you want that success! Choices enable our decisions. Choices impact every aspect of our lives, every minute of our day. Simply put, we choose every second of our waking hour, what we focus on, what we do, what we say. We choose how we react to every given situation. So those choices influence our thoughts, feelings and actions. Isn't it important, therefore, to always choose carefully?

Making a big life decision is pretty scary. But, know what's even scarier? Regret. A year from now, don't wish you had started today. Imagine what you want to see when you look into your rear view mirror in years to come. One day your life will flash before your eyes. Make sure it's worth watching!

Review of Chapter 4

1. What was your biggest insight whilst you were reading this chapter?
2. What decisions are you currently procrastinating over?
3. Why?
4. What is happening in your life right now, for which you need to take responsibility?
5. How many times are you prepared to accept a 'no' before you get one 'yes'?
6. Are you ready to accept change in your life?
7. Everyone has the resources within them to achieve the true potential! Do you?
8. What action will you take now after reading this chapter?

Definition of Success

Success: Living your life according to your highest values. When you dare to follow your dreams and enjoy the journey towards what you truly want instead of moving away from what you don't want.

Erdero Holland. (Robbie). Transformational Coach

Chapter 5
What's Stopping You?

"With realization of one's own potential and self confidence in one's ability, one can build a better world."
- Dalai Lama

The Critical Confidence Construct™ provides you with a model to help you identify what is stopping you, and overcome those challenges, obstacles and limiting beliefs.

Self-Aware

Know yourself. It is imperative to have a conscious awareness of your own thoughts, feelings, behaviours and motives, what influences them, the reasons why and, also, how. This brings together an understanding of your character, why you do or say certain things, or react in a particular way. This is the ability to be introspective. Whilst it may not always be pleasant to look within yourself, and learn and understand the real truth about yourself, your character and your drivers, with pure honesty, what it will do is lead to greater self-awareness. This will empower you with a greater degree of control in your life, something we explored in the previous chapter, to be able to adapt and react in the most appropriate ways to achieve your desired outcomes.

It is important to know and understand what makes you tick. What triggers different emotions within you. And why. The reason this is important? Well, put simply, once you have a greater awareness of yourself, you are in a position to exercise greater control over yourself. This brings more certainty into your life, in how you choose to react to situations, that is, your immediate thought processes, which in turn impact your feelings, and ultimately your behaviours. This is the simple cause and effect theory; master it rather than be a victim.

For example, a colleague may constantly make derogatory remarks to you, about your ability to do your job well. Imagine how this might make you feel. Do you believe it, do you begin to doubt yourself, when previously you considered yourself an over-performer? Does this knock your confidence? And how do you then react to that situation? You may decide to prove them wrong by pushing yourself even more, or conversely, you may accept that they are right, that you are not so great at your job, and in turn this begins to adversely affect your performance at work, and the situation generally creates for an unpleasant working environment. In this example, knowing yourself, being self aware, is likely to result in a positive outcome. Firstly, you are confident in your abilities to do an outstanding job, others' comments are unlikely to upset you and therefore to influence your behaviour, or your reaction to it. The comments would probably go over your head; you might even conclude that your colleague is seeking to put you down for the purposes of their own self-promotion; that's their issue, not yours.

"Keep away from small people who try to belittle your ambitions. Small people always do that, but the really great make you feel that you, too, can become great."
- Mark Twain

When you are in control, and aware of how you tick, you are in a strong position to manage situations that arise, and derive better outcomes. To the contrary, if you lacked any self-awareness, you would constantly be in reactionary mode, reacting to situations without thinking, without that deeper level of self that enables you to stop and consider, before responding. Further, your awareness of yourself enables you to better manage your state, positively impacting all areas of your life.

Think about everyday situations that send your blood pressure raging; road rage and the driver that cuts you up on the way to work. Be aware of you, manage your state, manage your reaction to the situation, and there is a far higher probability that you will arrive at work with a calm and positive outlook on the day ahead. How does this compare, in the same scenario, to where you immediately react with anger, start to wave abusive signs at the driver, and shout and hurl abuse at the driver (even though they cannot hear you); by the time you arrive at the office, what state are you in? Are you angry, annoyed, frustrated, wound up, about to explode…or all of these? How will that manifest with you for the remainder of the day? Will that be productive for you? Who has been affected by your reaction in both scenarios? Only you.

The ability to maintain an optimal state of mind is one of the most powerful strengths you can have. This defines you and your outcomes, in everything you do, say and feel. You can wake on a Monday morning, and that initial self-talk in your head sets the tone for the rest of the day. So whether you choose positive or negative self talk is up to you; you have a choice. And maintaining that state of mind requires you to become best friends with you, to explore and understand the rationale for your thoughts, feelings and behaviours. Once you have grasped the hang of this, the world is your oyster! You have the power to influence your everyday outcomes.

"I think self-awareness is probably the most important thing
towards becoming a champion."
- Billie Jean King

Self-Realisation

As you develop your conscious ability to know you, and why you do, say and feel certain things, you may want to change or adapt aspects of this, to unlearn some of your earlier experiences and behaviours. This is where you begin to explore at a subconscious level, the influences whilst you were growing up, be that from friends, family, or society in general. Without self-realisation, you will never fully understand your limits, nor be able to address them, overcome them and push yourself towards fulfilling your true potential.

Perhaps you repeatedly heard messages at school from your teachers, that your aspirations were beyond your reach, that you should accept and make do; perhaps you were made to feel that you weren't good enough. And as you grew up and progressed through your career, something was always holding you back, preventing you from pushing yourself to the next level.

Or maybe the messaging and conditioning that influenced you in your early years, the expectations others had of you, of what you would become, of the lifestyle you would live, has stopped you from really challenging yourself to achieve your true potential, to be truly fulfilled and happy. Perhaps you have achieved more than you set out to, way beyond your expectations, in terms of the success you defined for yourself early on. So now you have reached a plateau and don't know where to go next. Have you ever asked yourself, "What if I achieved so much more?" Imagine, how would that feel to you, what would it look like, and what would you hear?

Is it self-talk that is holding you back? For whatever reason, maybe you have a lot of self-doubt and negative chatter going on in your head. Others are better than you, you are not good enough, you don't deserve more, your biggest fear is of failure (feedback), or of success…which inevitably comes with responsibility. Perhaps you are insecure due to your own perception of yourself; for example, your background, where you came from, your family, or maybe it's your perception of your abilities, others' perceptions of you, challenges that you struggled to overcome, results you have had in the past which reinforce existing beliefs. Let's face it, how often has someone paid you a compliment, and it has totally made your day, changed your mood, popped a smile on your face, and inherently changed your overall state and attitude in a massively positive way? So why is it that you struggle to create your own positive self-talk, talk that will catapult you forward, that will inspire and encourage you to do greater things? Are you sabotaging your own success?

Fears: of failure, the unknown and risk

Although there are several factors that often hold people back from taking action, some of the more common reasons are a fear of failure, of the unknown, and of taking a risk. Thus avoiding disappointment, embarrassment and rejection, even getting hurt. Fear is one of the most common reasons for not taking action. Much of it is also self-created as we imagine and visualize negative outcomes. Which means that we can imagine and visualize positive outcomes!

When you truly know your purpose, your why, as long as you have the certainty and belief in your outcomes, and in your ability to execute on your plans, who is to say that you shouldn't go for it?

Are you worried about failing? In my view there is no such thing as failure, only feedback. If you have never failed, you have never tried anything new. The URL to be found at the link to my free bonuses will take you to a powerful 3-minute video on You Tube. It is definitely worth a look. It demonstrates just how self-belief, tenacity and determination empower people to achieve their outcomes, irrespective of the rejections or the negative feedback they receive.

Always expect criticism and negativity from those around you, when you set out to take action, especially if it's something new. Learn to differentiate between constructive and destructive criticism. Something that often holds people back is the thoughts and opinions others have of them. But why? Why care about the thoughts and opinions of others? More often than not, negative comments from others feed their own insecurities, their own lacking. If you succeed, you may leave them behind, possibly feeling inadequate, a failure, even jealous. That is not your problem to solve.

"Don't be distracted by criticism. Remember the only taste of success some people get, is taking a bite out of you."
- Zig Ziglar

Remember, focus on your outcomes, those that are congruent with your purpose and your why. Don't let others hold you back. You may be the only person who believes in you; but if you don't, who else will? Get out and do it anyway. Make a decision. Begin. Take action. And value the feedback that you receive. Then go take action again. Everything we want is on the other side of fear!

"Stop letting people who do so little for you, control so much of your mind, feelings and emotions."
- Will Smith

Self-Belief

In this chapter we have explored the importance of being self-aware, managing your state, and what triggers your behaviours. Then we have examined what may be holding you back, or stopping you from moving forward, how these thoughts may have been created, and how all these factors can influence your outcome. Now we will look at your belief in yourself, the degree of certainty you have in your abilities to achieve your purpose, your outcomes.

"When you develop yourself to the point where your belief in yourself is so strong that you know you can accomplish anything you put your mind to, you future will be unlimited."
- Brian Tracy

What drives your thoughts and behaviours? What influences what you think and how you feel? And what ultimately impacts what you do? Beliefs. Beliefs create certainty. Beliefs are incredibly powerful, so much so that they can empower you or disempower you in a second. You can develop beliefs about anything, so long as you have an element of certainty behind your belief.

It is important to look inside yourself, and the beliefs that you have learnt over the years, and to be critical with yourself, determining which beliefs serve you and which beliefs disempower you. This will require much introspection, and honesty with yourself. Examine why you made certain decisions in the past, or took certain actions and not others. What beliefs were these decisions and actions based on? Were those beliefs reflected in your outcomes?

Have you experienced a time when you have held a belief that was so deep-rooted that the outcome was inevitable? For example, you knew with absolute certainty that you would pass that exam, or get that job, or receive recognition for a great project at work? What about negative beliefs? Times when you knew with absolute certainty that you wouldn't get that promotion, that the presentation would go badly, or that you would miss that critical deadline? Beliefs influence our behaviours, thereby creating the actual fact, which is why it is so critical in order to achieve your outcomes that you believe in yourself, in your abilities, in your desired outcomes. Believe that you CAN do it! Any amount of self-doubt is opportunity for self-sabotage. And this must be avoided at all costs if you really want to succeed.

And where does the certainty come from? Perhaps your experiences – for example, maybe you tried to lose weight, you didn't reach your goal, and concluded that you cannot lose weight. Or perhaps you went for a promotion, and didn't get it. And concluded that you're not good enough.

So what messages are we running internally? The certainty behind our beliefs lies in the messages we tell ourselves, whether they are of our own creation, or from external influences. Maybe comments and opinions from your family, friends or teachers, whilst you were growing up. Off the cuff comments from your colleagues or acquaintances. So whether it's external messaging, or those that we tell ourselves, those beliefs create the facts, the certainty within our minds.

Remember, however, that you do have a choice. As to what you believe. As to what messages you are telling yourself. As to whether you choose to believe the empowering messages, or adopt those that may disempower you. And however challenging you may find this to begin with, keep repeating it, keep applying it, and soon it will become a habit. You won't even have to consciously think about it. You will naturally deliver compelling empowering messages to yourself all the time. In the meantime, simply act as if; that is, act as if you will achieve your outcome. In fact, imagine that you already have your outcome, that you have overcome your fears and insecurities. As you continue to act it, it will become habit-forming. You will believe it!

With greater self-awareness, something that you can develop over time, as well as the realization of what may be holding you back - fears you have developed over time, challenges to overcome, insecurities, obstacles in the mind - you can manage your state, i.e. your thoughts (which influence your feelings and behaviours) to turn any negative thoughts into positive messaging, which will empower you with the ability to believe in yourself, in your abilities, in your outcomes. You will discover a newly found freedom! You will have accomplished great breakthroughs! Remember, every one of us is unique, and yet, why do so many of us try so hard to fit in, when we were born to stand out?! Go for what you believe in!

"Your belief determines your action and your action determines your results, but first you have to believe."
- Mark Victor Hansen

Activity:

If you give up the following, you will start to experience massive change in your everyday life!! Give these up, even one per week, and keep a journal of the changes you start to notice in your day-to-day life;

1. Negative thinking – the minute your mind goes into negative thinking mode, STOP and correct yourself!

2. Negative self-talk – you decide to do something, and that negative chit-chat kicks off in your head, instilling self-doubt – STOP and create positive self talk!

3. Fear of failure – Write down a list of things you are afraid to do, and the outcomes you imagine which are holding you back. STOP! Now visualize positive successful outcomes in you mind, and embrace the feelings associated with your new vision.

4. Fear of success

5. Doubting yourself and your abilities

6. Criticising yourself

7. Procrastination

8. Caring what other people think

9. Living by other people's rules

Review of Chapter 5

1. What was your biggest insight whilst you were reading this chapter?
2. What triggers negative reactions in you?
3. What triggers positive reactions in you?
4. How would you feel if you could achieve so much more than you currently have? (this is measured by your own definition of success)
5. What are your 3 biggest fears?
6. List 5 beliefs you hold about yourself – then ask yourself why
7. Carry out the activity at the end of the chapter – give up those 9 habits!
8. What action will you take now after reading this chapter?

Definition of Success

Success for me is a continuum, an holistic achievement of outcomes that are special and unexpected.

It is a continuum as it is made up of small steps of achievement resulting in an end state that represents a position beyond my plans or expectations. In short I see small steps of success, but I cannot claim to be successful.

It is an holistic achievement as it cannot exist with just one aspect of my life; I can only can claim success if I have achieved what is important to me in all key areas of my life – being my family, my relationships, my faith and my work.

The achievement that represents success is something that is 'special' because it matters to me (it may have little relevance to someone else) – a work achievement will matter more to me if I initiated the outcome rather than delivered on someone else's plan. Something is 'special' to me, not because of position or title but because of my unique contribution.

It will be unexpected because I have surprised myself and delivered at levels I had not expected, thus bringing higher personal satisfaction.

Andrew Jones, VP Finance Region Controllership

Chapter 6
Love It When a Plan Comes Together!

"A goal without a plan is just a wish."

So far in this book we have examined the steps that you need to master, the laying of the foundations, in order to get you from where you are to where you want to be. So armed with your "Why?" – your purpose, your positive attitude, masses of energy generated from your newly implemented health and wellbeing habits – and having taken control of you, with your awareness of what makes you tick, and insurmountable self-belief, what happens next? It's time to look at the implementation, your Compelling Commitment Creator™. First comes the planning, towards achieving your goals. Without planning, a goal is just a wish.

I have created seven steps within the planning tool. This tool is designed to ensure your goal is compelling because, if it isn't, your incentive to follow through will be challenging in itself. A plan has no value unless you are prepared to put in the hard work and effort to execute it. When setting goals, it is important to identify the compelling reasons to follow through. Otherwise it will be very easy to give up at the first hurdle.

Rationale

"A person will more likely to commit to an activity once they understand the rationale behind it."

Once you have identified your goal, consider the ecology surrounding the achievement of this goal; in other words, how will achieving your goal impact those around you, your family, friends and colleagues, for example? If you had aspirations to get that promotion, but accepting it meant relocating to another continent, who would this impact? And would those impacted be happy with the opportunity to move? What if one of those people had a close relative nearby who was seriously unwell? Would they be okay with upping sticks to move to the other side of the world? Would there be an impact to children and their schooling? Would grandparents become distraught due to the distance that would be created?

All of these are life-changing considerations, to determine whether the goal itself is rational, what the impact of achieving it would be, to both yourself, your family and friends, and others around you. Contrast this with the impact of not achieving the goal; how would you feel, how would this look for you and what would you hear? Essentially you are weighing the pros and cons of striving to achieve this goal with foregoing it if it isn't congruent with your wider goals for you and those who are important in your life.

Relevance

"Identify those successes that really matter to you."

Consider how congruent your goal is with your purpose, your "why?" Does your goal form part of your priorities? Is it important for you to achieve this goal? What would happen if you didn't achieve it? What impact would that have on your life? Does the goal align with your values? And does this goal represent your vision of where you want to be, or take you a step closer, to some degree? Finally, does the thought of achieving this goal fill you with passion? You may set yourself a goal just because it sounds like a great thing to do; however, examining the relevance to your overall purpose will determine how driven and focused you will be to achieve it, how meaningful the outcome would be for you. The extent of the relevance will also suggest how prepared you may be to give up if it becomes challenging, how easy it would be to walk away. If your goal and the actions you are taking are not closely aligned with your purpose, it will be far easier to give up, if it is requiring exerted effort. On the other hand, if the goal is congruent with where you are heading, you will be more likely to push yourself, to exert the extra effort and energy, to find a way to overcome any obstacles to keep you moving forward.

Realistic

"I am realistic; I expect miracles."
- Wayne Dyer

How realistic is it for you to achieve this goal? Do you have the skillset, the capabilities, the knowledge? Do you have a support group around you that you can turn to, for guidance, direction or general morale boosting? If not, that's okay. You can go learn, develop and grow. That's good too. How much time would you need to invest to be armed with the tools and strategies to make it happen? And where in your typical day can you carve out the time to assign to this personal growth and development? The relevance, which we discussed above, will define how much you are prepared to compromise, to sacrifice, to commit, in order to grow, in order to fulfill your goal. In other words, if you need to invest time in developing yourself with the skills, etc., towards achieving your goal, how can you create the time to do so? And how committed will you be to pursuing that? The relevance will define that. What is an unrealistic goal?

This could be a goal you set yourself, in the full knowledge that there are obstacles and hurdles that you absolutely must overcome in order to get you there. That doesn't mean it isn't possible. However, the reality of achieving it must be assessed against those hurdles, and how willing and determined you are to overcome those. If the drive and determination isn't there, the goal becomes unrealistic and you are setting yourself up for failure.

Responsible

"Accept responsibility for your life. Know that it is you who will get you where you want to go, no one else."
- Les Brown

Take responsibility. Make a commitment to yourself. Own your life, your decisions and your outcomes. Before you begin to blame everyone and everything around you, when things go wrong, they don't work out, or your outcome isn't as planned, take a decision that you are fully responsible for your life, and that you will take control, make decisions, and follow through. You will not be dependent upon others; instead you will be entirely independent and in charge of where your journey is taking you. You will grab the bull by the horns and manoeuvre it in the direction that you wish to go. You will overcome setbacks, circumvent obstacles, and keep focused on your desired outcome. Failure to achieve your outcome is simply feedback for you to go for it again, and learn from what went wrong. As long as you have the commitment to follow through, to never give up, and to apply yourself 100% to whatever you are focused on at that time, to actively take responsibility for your outcomes and ensuring they are congruent with your purpose, you are 100 times closer than the next person to achieving them.

Recognisable

"Measured progress inspires!"

How will you know whether you achieved your desired outcomes? When you set your goals, you need to be clear on your desired outcomes. So how do you go about measuring this? Unless you have specific black and white results, facts and figures for example, you must derive other measurables. The way in which you go about this is to set your goal, be clear on your outcome, and then, consider how you would feel upon achieving this. What would that outcome look like for you? What would you see? And what would you hear? What messages will you be telling yourself?

Remember, you want to push yourself to your maximum, to achieve your absolute potential, so when considering your feelings, what it will look like and what you will hear, you may find yourself having different ratings depending on the levels of your outcome. And the ratings are dependent also on how far you are prepared to push yourself, to get up and try again, how much you are prepared to challenge yourself, and how determined you are to achieve your desired end result!

You may set yourself a goal to lose 14 pounds in weight, but you plateau having lost 10 pounds, and decide that you are satisfied with that. However, the feelings you experience, what you will see, and your internal messaging, may likely be quite different at the 10 pound mark, than if you had achieved your ultimate goal of 14 pounds. And this is why it is important at the outset to decide where you really want to be, where you want to get to, and create those measurables to assist you in knowing when you get there. Of course, you can decide that the 10 pounds is okay; your own success is personal to you.

However, what you are seeking to avoid is having regret, so it is at this stage that you make a decision as to whether you are truly satisfied with where you are (10 pounds lost) or whether it is an absolute must (for whatever reason – it's personal to you) to push yourself that extra mile to shift the last few pounds. There is no right or wrong answer; it is entirely up to you. However, you know the feelings you experience, what you see and your internal messaging, at the 10 pound stage, and then it's for you to decide whether you are content with that, or you want to push yourself more.

Run Time

"Time is the scarcest resource,
and unless it is managed nothing else can be managed."
- Peter Drucker

A plan needs a deadline. Without this, you could continue indefinitely to work on your plan to achieve your goals, and very easily lose momentum. It is also easy to lose focus and commitment, when the time invested working towards that goal becomes indefinite. Some people find that they work better under pressure, so depending on the goal itself, you may find that as the deadline looms, you become more focused, motivated and determined! On the other hand, you may be someone who needs to create a detailed plan, breaking the goal down into small tasks, assigning time to each task, and then figuring out how to adapt your current time pressures to accommodate these tasks.

Time management becomes critical here. We talked earlier about being realistic, and about the time available to expend towards your efforts. In saying this, if you want an outcome so bad, you will find a way. You made that decision, you want that outcome. Now it's just about figuring out how. There may be mini-outcomes along the way, which go a long way to keeping us motivated and progressing in the right direction. We also need to consider our priorities, as well as dependencies within that specific goal. Depending upon the outcome, there may be a number of actions that you can run in parallel, so with time being your limiting factor, you need to prioritise those actions. And then you have dependencies. There may be actions that are dependent upon completing another action first. So your time management requires careful thought.

Create a detailed planner, firstly identifying all the steps, the actions, required to achieve your outcome, identifying the dependencies, prioritizing different components. Then create a time planner (or use your existing diary or agenda) to schedule in slots of time, which will be solely devoted to working on your actions, your steps needed to achieve your outcomes. Now given the busy lives that we all lead, you may well look at your existing commitments and decide that you simply cannot schedule in time for this goal, that there are simply no gaps.

If this occurs, you need to revisit the rationale for having this goal, and your desire for the outcome. In addition, how relevant is this goal to your overall purpose? Is it realistic, achievable; are there many challenges to overcome to get you there? Are you taking full responsibility for achieving your desired outcome? And are you clear on how you will measure your achievements? Once you have revisited these, ask yourself, how much do you really want this? What are you prepared to do, to sacrifice, to compromise on, to get you there? The answer may be nothing. And that is okay, as long as you know that you made that decision, and you are happy to live with the consequences and the feelings of not having achieved that goal. Perhaps the outcome of that particular goal isn't a priority for you, or is not in alignment with your overall vision of where you want to be.

On the other hand, you may be willing to move heaven and earth to get there. The likelihood then is that your goal is in true alignment with your purpose.

In this case, you will look at your current weekly/monthly schedule, and examine where you are spending your time. And I mean, do this in detail. So be accountable for every hour of every day. Perhaps you spend 8 hours sleeping, 3 hours preparing meals and eating, an hour for showering, dressing etc. and 2 hours commuting, along with 8 hours at work. That leaves you with 2 hours remaining in your day. How do you currently spend them? Perhaps you exercise, or you watch TV, spend time with your children, chat on the phone to friends, or check out what everyone else is doing on social media. So now it's about prioritizing what you currently do, looking for ways to be more time-efficient and productive, and looking at what really adds value to your life, what are you doing that is moving you forward, developing you, and taking you towards where you want to be. Remove anything that adds no value. Then consider areas where you can compromise. Perhaps you can manage on one hour less sleep. Or prepare dinner for 2 or3 days at a time so that frees up time a couple evenings from preparation. You may find that you really need to be disciplined with yourself in this exercise. Time management is one of the biggest challenges we face in today's society. Be mindful of demands that are draining on your energy and time.

Reward

"Celebrate your accomplishments, however small."

Rewarding yourself every step of the way on your journey to where you want to be will keep you motivated and keep your morale high. Celebrate your accomplishments along the way;

this provides you a mini-break on the journey, keeps you on an emotional and mental high and re-energises you to keep going.

Celebrating creates a commitment towards your personal growth. Taking time during those celebrations to reflect on your journey, to gain valuable insights, can instill greater confidence and push you towards creating bigger goals. Reflection will help you to define what brought about that success and will create learnings for the future; what worked well, and identifying areas for improvement. You may even ask yourself whether you can perhaps achieve more than you originally set out to.

Without rewarding yourself along your journey towards your ultimate goal, the process may seem like a long hard slog, with the celebrations almost beyond reach, and creates a reason to want to give up. So when you are creating your plan and have identified all the sub-steps, and actions to get you to your goal, also consider how you can reward yourself with small treats and celebrations, the carrot to keep you going to the next level.

Let's look at an example of how we would encapsulate these planning steps into creating the journey towards your end goal. Let's say that your end goal is to improve your general health and wellbeing.

Rationale: Examine how achieving this goal will affect you and those around you. Is it a step that enables you in some way to move towards where you want to be in life? Are there any adverse implications of pursuing this goal? Broadly speaking, it is unlikely that striving for improved health will have an adverse impact on you or those around you. However, do consider the impact of how you plan to achieve your goal. You may decide that you will dedicate two hours a day every weeknight towards training and exercise; what are you compromising on or giving up to achieve this? It may not sit comfortably with your partner if, for example, you have a newborn or young child, and the time that you would usually have spent with your child (and given your partner a break) is now replaced with a training regime, or you are building a relationship with a partner who suddenly learns that you won't be around 5 nights a week.

Relevant: Is your goal congruent with your purpose? Given the nature of this goal, and the benefits of having optimal health and wellbeing in general, it is safe to say that this goal is aligned with your life purpose, and will provide you the energy and focus to get you to where you want to be.

Realistic: Optimal health is achievable for anyone, albeit the measure of optimal may vary by individual, based on their starting point and any health challenges they have or need to overcome. In this case it is about setting realistic goals that, once achieved, will incentivize you to create a bigger goal. The ability to achieve the goal in this case is greatly attributed to mindset; however, you can, of course, train to develop specific skills, should you desire. With this goal, as with any, it is important to set realistic goals that are achievable, with a view to creating a bigger goal thereafter, as it is so easy to give up if you are not seeing results within a reasonable timeframe.

Responsible: This is about taking full responsibility for achieving your goal – own it! This is not a time for excuses and placing blame on others; for example, it was someone's birthday party, or a hen/stag do so I had to eat badly and drink lots. I am not saying you cannot have a day off; however, that is not an excuse for not starting, or for extending bad habits for an entire week! Or, I am so busy at work, I don't have the time to train; you can find 20-30 minutes in a day to walk, albeit in short bursts of 5 to 10 minutes, taking the stairs rather than the lifts, all small actions which add up towards your daily goal. You results are up to you; make that commitment to yourself to follow through!

Recognisable: How do you measure your goals, to know that you are making progress? Within this goal, you may have created mini goals, with respect to your weight, your energy levels, a change in eating habits, how your clothes fit, how you look. Weight is black and white. You may decide you wish to lose 14 pounds (a stone); however, if you could lose 10 pounds you would still be happy. Will you be satisfied with that outcome, with how you feel, what you see and your internal messaging? How would that differ from achieving the loss of 14 pounds? This is an example of having different ratings subject to your outcome.

Energy levels may be measured by how you feel, perhaps first thing in the morning, the time you usually struggle to get going, or mid afternoon when typically your energy levels begin to flag. And how would that look for you? Maybe you see yourself running for longer, or further, perhaps training more intensely in the gym, or getting more done, being more productive, simply because you have more energy. These are all measures of achievement.

How will you track your eating habits to know you are on track? Perhaps applying the 80/20 Pareto principle may help; 80% of the time you eat well, with no processed and unhealthy foods, sugar fuelled drinks, caffeine etc and 20% of the time, you simply eat and drink what you want, say on weekends or when you are out at social events. This also helps to maintain realistic goals, and may remove the cravings as well as the guilt. Again, create measures that will align with how you want to feel about your achievement.

What about how your clothes fit? What is the measure? Perhaps you can fit into two sizes smaller than previously. However, this is relative, and perhaps you know full well you can drop another 3 or more dress sizes. How do you see yourself once you have achieved your goal? Will be you be satisfied and content having dropped 2 sizes or do you feel unsettled until you lose another 3? These feelings, what you see and what you hear, once you accomplish your goals, drive your measure of success, whatever success means for you.

Runtime: Your starting point, your intended end result, the challenges you have to overcome and the hurdles you need to surpass, as well as the reality of the time you have available to dedicate to this goal, will all determine your time schedule and timeline to accomplish this goal. Be realistic with yourself. Don't over-stretch yourself and over-commit, only to find that you are failing to maintain your schedule, which in turn will dampen your motivation and risk you giving up. If you need to create a longer, more realistic timeline to achieve your end goal, do so. At least this way you will more likely maintain momentum.

Reward: Create little rewards along the way as you journey to your goal of ultimate health and wellbeing. That doesn't mean going to the extreme and eating and drinking to your heart's content for a week, thereby cancelling out any progress you had made up until that point! You can, however, treat yourself (still applying the 80/20 rule for example); treat yourself to a spa day, take a few hours to chill out with a good book or movie, go shopping for a new outfit to show off your new figure; anything that feels like a celebration of your progress and will drive you towards achieving your end goal!

"Success doesn't just happen. It's planned for!"

Review of Chapter 6

1. What was your biggest insight whilst you were reading this chapter?
2. Identify a goal that you have, and explore the rationale for pursuing it
3. How congruent is your goal with your purpose?
4. What is the reality of you achieving this goal - what do you need to do to ensure absolute success?
5. Own your goal and your outcome!
6. How will you measure your levels of success?
7. What is your timeline to achieve your goal?
8. How will you celebrate your success?
9. What action will you take now after reading this chapter?

Definition of Success

"Success is deciding what you want, breaking it down into smaller outcomes and then doing them."

Andy Harrington,
Founder of The Professional Speakers Academy

Chapter 7
Just Do It!

Having examined your goal, ensuring that it is compelling enough to enable you with the requisite commitment and momentum to follow through, you now step into execution mode, your Supreme Success Strategy™.

1. Firstly you begin with RESEARCH: this is where you identify what you need to enable you to reach your goal. Depending on your goal, your familiarity with the territory and whether this is something you have done before, research could be a short exercise or it may take some time.

If your goal is, for example, making a career change, there will be research needed to understand the requirements, skills and abilities of successful people in similar careers or roles. A great way to achieve success is to model other successful people. So perhaps you can identify a successful person who is achieving success doing what you want to do, be that in a specific career, business, or in health and wellness. For example, you could identify a sports icon that you admire, or an executive of a large corporation. Once you identify that person, you study them, their strategies, what they do, have done, and how, and understand what makes them successful, to enable you to accomplish whatever it is that you admire in them.

If you are looking to break into a new sector or industry, this will require research to better understand that, as well as the language used, the experience and qualifications you may need, the types of people you are up against – again, consider identifying one of the best in the field to model. If you aspire to move to another country, you will need to have done your research, both in terms of the requirements to relocate abroad, as well as gaining an understanding of local culture, language, traditions, food, cost of living, etc. Speak to others who have achieved something similar, or are doing what you want to do; ask questions and gain knowledge and advice; draw on the resources around you.

Have you got all the resources you require? How do you view your current ability to execute your goal? What skills do you need, and do you currently possess these at the levels necessary to execute your plan? Or do you need to upskill? If so, how will you go about this? How much investment is required, in time and money? Having already looked at where you spend your time, you have an idea of how much time you can attribute to working towards your goal, which in turn will give you an indication of your timelines to get you ready with the appropriate levels of skills and abilities to achieve your best outcomes.

2. Once you are armed with all the information you need, it's time to CONSOLIDATE this. The output of your research forms the structure of your plan. Now you are clear on where you need to be, in order to achieve your goal; the skills set, abilities, knowledge, qualifications and training, the network you need to build, risks involved, financial investment, time needed to complete various activities where you have been able to identify this, etc.

At this point you can create a list of all this information, perhaps in subsections, for example, (1) Skills and Abilities (2) Qualifications and Training (3) Network: who I need to know (4) Risks (5) Financials

3. Now its time to FORMULATE your plan! With the consolidation of all your research, you need to generate a plan of action, which is all the steps, actions, to-do's, whatever you like to call it. Again, you can create these in subsections, and try to make them as granular as possible. The reason I say this is that, often, people create an action which is so high-level that, when they look at it later, it just feels so overwhelming and subsequently procrastination sets in.

For example ' File paperwork'; when you see this, your heart sinks, you envision that towering pile of months worth of papers, and the thought of tackling it seems impossible; where to start, it will take hours…and then you put it off for another time. Maybe if you were to break the task down into sub-tasks, you could spend a short 30 minutes completing one of those. Think, 'task 1 – separate mountain into separate piles, for utility bills, bank statements, credit card statements, tax documents/payslips etc'; 'task 2 – review one pile, action and file accordingly', and so it goes on. Slowly you will make progress through what first seemed an overwhelming task! That would give you a great feeling of completion and of making progress, and inspire you to keep going.

So break down your actions into the smallest tasks. There is a huge feeling of satisfaction derived from completing even the smallest task, and ticking it off your list, which in turn inspires you to complete another task.

4. Once you have a list of actions, you need to PRIORITISE them. Create a timeline for them. Identify the approximate time required to complete each action, identify those actions which you can run in parallel (for example, you may have different workstreams) and those actions which are dependent upon completion of another. Identify those tasks that are important over those that are merely urgent, and don't let others determine your use of time. Remain in control. Create your timeline in a format you are comfortable working with; it could be a written list, a diagram, on paper or online, as long as it is a working document that you are happy with using daily. Align your timeline with your personal calendar, diary, agenda, whatever you typically use on a day-to-day basis. We talked earlier about identifying the hours available to invest in working towards your goal, so if you have 2 hours per day available to devote to your goal, reflect this in your action timeline. This way, you can see realistically how long it will take you to accomplish your goal. And if you are not happy with what you see; for example, it is taking too long to complete an activity, you can adjust your diary to free up more time, in turn enabling you to complete your task sooner.

5. Now its time for the fun part! Execute!! Begin taking ACTION!! Small steps towards your big goal. You are on your journey to achieve your desired outcomes!! Invest the requisite time and energy to complete each action.

Having taken the time to examine your why, your purpose, aligning this with your goals and desired outcomes; adopted the mindset to get you there, instilling energy and focus by striving towards achieving optimal health; made a decision to take control of your life, embrace change and explore your choices; challenged your beliefs, becoming more self-aware; and developing self assurance, created a compelling plan that ensures you will maintain the momentum to get you to where you want to be, and now formulated a detailed plan, it's time for execution!

All the preparation should position you with the confidence, dedication and commitment to follow through on your action plan, however challenging it may seem. Yes, there is always the option to give up, and that is the point at which you revert back to imagining those feelings you will experience, what you will see, how it will look for you, and what you will hear when you achieve your goal, and contrasting that with the feelings you will experience, what you will see and hear, were you to give up on your goal. This will empower you to keep going, keep pushing yourself, investing 100% of your internal resources, to move you towards your outcomes. Because you know, without a doubt, that you can do it! You have made a decision, as well as taken absolute responsibility, to achieve your outcome. So, what's stopping you?

6. What were your RESULTS? What was the outcome you achieved? Was it as you had imagined when you set out to take action? What feedback have you received? What, if anything, didn't go as planned? Your results are also reflected in the way you feel, how the outcome looks for you, and what you hear. Are these aligned with what you had expected when you envisaged achieving your goal? If not, can you identify the gaps? For example, you anticipated that you would experience certain feelings and emotions upon accomplishing your goal. However, they are not as expected. Ask yourself why. Has anything changed since you set your goal? How big is the gap between how you feel in reality and what you had anticipated feeling? Perhaps the goal wasn't as challenging as you had imagined, and so the feelings you expected, perhaps of huge elation at your accomplishment, just aren't there. There may be several reasons. Take the time and seek to understand why the gap has arisen.

7. REVIEW your results. Are you satisfied with your outcome, with your progress? If not, why? Has your goal been achieved? If the answer is no, explore the reasons why. What obstacles did you encounter? What challenges did you overcome? And how could you have executed better on your actions? Always be looking for ways to improve so, even if you have achieved your outcome, and the result couldn't have been better, there is always learning to take away, which you can use in the future. If you smashed your goal, achieved an outcome you wouldn't have dreamt of, that's amazing! Still take the time to review what you did, the why, the how, and learn from your experiences.

8. And finally…REFINE. Take your experiences and look to refine your approach, be that on the same goal or a future one. You are always learning, always growing, and it is this reflection on your experiences and the actions you took that will empower you with the tools and strategies to keep achieving, to keep moving forward, and to gradually achieve success, as defined by you, in all areas of your life.

"I dream, I test my dreams against my beliefs, I take risks, and I execute my vision to make those dreams come true."
- Walt Disney

Review of Chapter 7

1. What was your biggest insight whilst you were reading this chapter?
2. Undertake research towards achieving your goal
3. Consolidate the output of your research to structure your plan
4. Create an action plan, detailing all the steps
5. Prioritise the steps, identifying interdependencies and steps that you can run in parallel
6. Execute on your plan – take action!
7. Obtain your results! What was the outcome?
8. Review your results – what lessons have you learned, what you be improved, are you satisfied with your outcome?
9. Refine your approach, for the same goal or a future one
10. What action will you take now after reading this chapter?

Definition of Success

I believe success is a by-product of the number of people you serve. Many people measure success by money and riches but money has no meaning but the one you attach to it.

Come from a place of "service" and shift the focus from 'you' onto 'others' instead. When you look back at how many lives you have changed, how many people you have inspired and the impact you have had on the world, you can hand on heart say you've been successful!

Learn to serve others and success will follow you in abundance!

Jessen James
Serial Entrepreneur, Business Mentor &
Multi Award Winning Speaker
www.jessenjames.com

Some Final Thoughts

I hope that reading Success Redefined has inspired you to search for your true purpose, to take action, to leverage your natural talents to become limitless!

And I hope I have achieved my purpose of having you stop and take time to really think about your life, your true purpose, to challenge yourself and your thought processes, to create your vision of the outcomes you really want in your life, and to empower you with the foundations – the mindset, energy and decision-making capabilities – to get you there, at the same time, challenging your beliefs and limitations, and creating a compelling plan to get you to where you want to be.

I wish for you that, upon completing this book, you walk away with a deep understanding of what really matters to you and why, and a belief that there are no limitations in achieving your ultimate success – whatever success may mean for you! My belief is that your only limitations are those you are telling yourself. We all have the resources within us to fulfill our potential. Nothing is stopping you, but you. Let's leverage your natural talents to become limitless!

If I can be of further assistance to you through my coaching programs, upcoming talks, seminars and workshops, I would be deeply honoured to be able to serve you once again. I look forward to meeting you and hearing about your successes in person. Until then, I wish you a happy, healthy and successful future!

Leila xxx

About the Author

Leila Singh was born in 1972 in London, England, to parents of Caribbean descent, (whose ancestors originated from India) who emigrated to London in 1961 from British Guiana, South America. Her father qualified as a Barrister at the Middle Temple, London in 1967, and her late mother held various telephonist roles over the years, latterly at the Metropolitan Police service in North-West London.

Leila qualified as an Accountant (FCCA) in 1997, after graduating from Oxford Brookes University three years earlier. Having started out working within an accounting practice, her early career was spent building her finance experience in a range of diverse roles within some great companies, including a leading Russian Steel Trading Company, a Top 6 multinational law firm (part of the Silver Circle of British law firms) and a global telecommunications company.

Since then, Leila has achieved great things in her diverse career, exceling in all her pursuits. She spent two years working in financial recruitment where she further developed her people skills and understanding of others' motivations and behaviours. It was during this time that Leila realized her passion for coaching others towards fulfilling their potential and achieving their aspirations, a passion which she finds truly rewarding.

Leila has developed her career in corporate finance and sales within a global IT company over the last 12 years, whilst pursuing her avid interest in personal development, including qualifying as an NLP Practitioner and Hypnotherapist in March 2014. Her NLP Master Practitioner will be completed in February 2016. In parallel she is currently working with highly motivated individuals like herself to uncover their own definition of success, get clarity on where they want to be, and overcome their perceived limitations to become limitless!

After learning through experience at a young age that pill popping wasn't the solution, Leila has overcome severe health challenges through simply practicing holistic health strategies consistently over the last 20 years. Her genuine interest and research into this area positions her with valuable and insightful knowledge on preventative methods to achieve and maintain optimal health.

Leila's journey has culminated in the writing of her first book, Success Redefined, where she shares the system she has created to achieve success, based on simple principles she has applied throughout her own life, and also with her coaching clients. She will get you out of your comfort zone, challenge you, and have you really search inside yourself to identify your true purpose, what makes you tick, what is holding you back, from getting to where you want to be. In addition, Leila considers health and wellbeing to be a critical factor in enabling ultimate success, notwithstanding the many other benefits of maintaining optimal health, and as such has included an entire module on 'Your Greatest Asset', health, within her system.

Leila is a source of inspiration. Her passion for life is infectious. With the end game in mind, her laser sharp focus, dedication and tenacity ensures that she delivers positive outcomes with authenticity and integrity. She is the consummate professional, highly motivated with a positive can-do attitude, whilst her warm and friendly style, puts others at ease.

Leila lives in London, and in her spare time enjoys keeping fit, watching cricket and tennis, travelling, spending time with family and friends, and drinking endless mugs of herbal tea!